The
JANE AUSTEN
Handbook

Library of Congress Cataloging in Publication Number:
2006938583

ISBN: 978-1-59474-171-5

Printed in China

Typeset in Caslon

Designed by Bryn Ashburn
Illustrations by Kathryn Rathke

Distributed in North America by Chronicle Books
85 Second Street
San Francisco, CA 94105

10 9 8 7 6 5 4 3 2 1

Quirk Books
215 Church Street
Philadelphia, PA 19106
www.quirkbooks.com

The
JANE AUSTEN
Handbook

A Sensible Yet Elegant Guide to Her World

By Margaret C. Sullivan

Illustrations by Kathryn Rathke

QUIRK BOOKS
PHILADELPHIA

For my mother,
who let me read
everything.

CONTENTS

INTRODUCTION

"If adventures will not befall a young lady in her own village, she must seek them abroad."
—JANE AUSTEN, *NORTHANGER ABBEY*

"What is it about Jane Austen, anyway?" All Janeites have heard the question at one time or another, whether from a friend, significant other, co-worker, parole officer, or a math teacher who caught said Janeite reading *Emma* under the desk during class. "She's been dead for two hundred years! She wrote stories about upper-class twits desperate to marry other upper-class twits! How can these books possibly be relevant to life in the twenty-first century?"

There really is no way to respond to such a question. How to explain the sheer tingling joy one experiences when two interesting, complex, and occasionally aggravating characters have at last settled their misunderstandings and will live happily ever after, no matter what travails life might throw in their path, because Jane Austen said they will, and that's that? How to describe the exhilaration of being caught up in an unknown but glamorous world of balls and gowns and rides in open carriages with handsome young men? How to explain that the best part of Jane Austen's world is that sudden recognition that the characters are *just like you*?

If you are nodding, Gentle Reader, this book is for you. We will not scold you for wanting to understand entailments and wedding clothes and the delicate politics of a ballroom. (Because it does rather bring the fantasy to a screeching halt to realize one is not familiar with the intricacies of, say, paying a morning call.) We will instead undertake to explain the mysteries of life among early nineteenth-century British landed gentry—mysteries that Jane Austen, writing for an audience of her contemporaries, did not find mysterious at all. Here are step-by-step instructions that will allow one to conduct one's fantasy life with perfect aplomb—or at least to better understand the background when Lizzy or Emma or Elinor or Catherine or Fanny or Anne are faced with a similar situation in the novels or films.

Have you ever wondered where Mr. Darcy got his riches—or how much that ten thousand a year would be worth today? Or why Emma Woodhouse looks down upon the Coxes but not on the Westons? Why Lady Russell spends every winter in Bath, or why Fanny Price was stuck in Portsmouth until someone male could come and take her away? These subjects, and others, are covered in the first section of this book, which deals with some of the logistical considerations of life among the gentry of Regency England.

The second section explores the ins and outs of how one spent one's day in a period when having an actual job was frowned upon, while in the third section, "Making Love" (stop giggling, you guttersnipes; the phrase meant something different then and you know it!), one will learn the all-important rules for choosing a prospective husband.

And as Mrs. Bennet pointed out in *Pride and Prejudice*, a family in a country estate can expect to dine with as many as four and twenty families, so one will wish to know how to conduct oneself in social interactions. The fourth section addresses the nagging questions on the intricacies of dancing, country house parties, and all manner of card games, including the ever-present, if not dreadfully boring, whist.

We also have included a short biography of Jane Austen; descriptions of her novels and the concoctions of modern Austen fans, such as films, sequels, and merchandise; and a handy glossary of the terms that have puzzled many modern readers.

Some might protest that the trappings of Jane Austen's world are unimportant—that only the story matters. Others might point out that life in Jane Austen's time was not all small beer and skittles—that intelligent and genteel young ladies were left impoverished, soldiers and sailors went off to war and did not return, and beloved authors fell ill and died too young.

But like Jane herself, I quit such odious subjects as soon as I can, and leave the pens of the many excellent Jane Austen scholars to dwell on guilt and misery. This book is for the Janeite who, while relatively content living in the modern world, indulges in the occasional unashamed wallow in Austenland. Who among us has not imagined being mistress (or master) of Pemberley, or a trim frigate, or even an unpretending parsonage? Come, confess!

As no less a philosopher than Miss Elizabeth Bennet pointed out, "the wife of Mr. Darcy must have such extraordinary sources of happiness necessarily attached to her situation, that she could, upon the whole, have no cause to repine." While the careful Janeite will remember the lesson of Catherine Morland in *Northanger Abbey*, who forgot that real life is not like books, even her very commonsense hero, Henry Tilney, admitted that it is only natural to be drawn to the charms of a well-written novel. Jane's novels are so true to life that even two centuries later they are fresh and funny and, yes, relevant as ever.

The carriage awaits, Gentle Reader. Will you step in, and let us take you on a great adventure?

—*The Authoress*

SECTION I:

Jane Austen's World & Welcome to It

How to

BECOME AN ACCOMPLISHED LADY

"It is amazing to me," said Bingley, "how young ladies can have patience to be so very accomplished as they all are. . . . They all paint tables, cover skreens, and net purses. I scarcely know any one who cannot do all this, and I am sure I never heard a young lady spoken of for the first time, without being informed that she was very accomplished." —PRIDE AND PREJUDICE

Well-bred young ladies must acquire a store of accomplishments that are of no practical use and are, therefore, quite attractive to gentlemen. However, one certainly is not born with the ability to play concertos upon the pianoforte, translate Italian love songs, paint tables, cover screens, net purses, and perform all the other talents of the accomplished lady. These skills are acquired through an intensive training process that begins in childhood and continues until the triumphant day of marriage, whereupon one can rest comfortably on one's laurels.

⚜ **Study several languages.** Become well-versed in French, certainly, and Italian, so you can read music and translate love songs. There is no need to learn Latin or Greek, however—you'll be thought a bluestocking.

⚜ **Acquire a basic grasp of geography and history.** One need only concentrate on the fundamentals in formal study, but if you want to learn more, the books in your father's library will provide an opportunity to do so.

Become a proficient musician. A lady who can sing and play upon the pianoforte, or better yet, the harp, will always attract a husband, because he'll think she will be able to entertain him and his guests in the evenings. Many women give up music entirely once they are married, but fortunately the gentlemen never seem to catch on.

Draw or paint the picturesque. Pencil drawing and watercolor painting are ladylike endeavors. Choose picturesque subjects for your art (see "The 'Picturesque,'" page 70): Concentrate on ruins (the more tumbledown the better); dead trees; and rough or rustic landscapes. If no picturesque elements are present in real life, add them from your imagination.

A GENTLEMAN'S EDUCATION

Boys learned to read and write from their parents, the family governess, or the village parson. Once they reached the age of ten, they received a more formal education in Latin and Greek, mathematics, history, and literature. Private tutors could be hired; these gentlemen might have several boys come to them or might live with a family like a male governess. Other boys attended a public school, such as Eton or Rugby.

A young man who wished to take holy orders, or who just liked learning, might have spent a few terms or earned a degree at Oxford or Cambridge. In the late eighteenth century, a young male heir to great estates embarked upon the "grand tour," a one- to five-year trip to the Continent, though this tradition was interrupted by the Napoleonic Wars from 1803 to 1815. He would learn languages and absorb culture, keep a travel diary, and acquire *objets d'art*.

Apprenticeships were available for young men destined for professions. Aspiring barristers could read law under a member of the bar. The Royal Navy took on boys as young as eight as unpaid "captain's servants," who would live aboard ship and learn the art of command. They would become midshipmen, the most junior officers, and work their way up the ranks.

◉ **Master the art of needlework.** To be an accomplished woman, you must know how to do fancy needlework as well as the more mundane aspects of sewing for the family, even though you will contract out the vast majority of the utilitarian work once you are married. A married woman's primary sewing tasks are to make her husband's shirts and cravats and do the family mending. When company is present, she will display impressive embroidery and decorative needle arts.

◉ **Learn to dance gracefully.** The ballroom is the center of a young lady's life. When you are not dancing at balls, you will no doubt be longing for the opportunity. Practice with your sisters until you are officially "out" (see "Coming Out," page 159).

A LADY'S EDUCATION

Most young women were educated by a combination of teachers, all working toward the ultimate goal of producing an elegant creature who would take the *ton* by storm— or at least escape becoming a spinster. Here are some of those responsible for her lessons.

- **Parents.** In some households, a girl's mother taught her to read and write and do basic arithmetic, and perhaps some rudimentary French. Her father also might have been involved in her instruction, particularly if he were a member of the clergy. This may have been all the formal education a young woman received, unless her parents hired a governess or sent her to school around age ten.

- **A governess.** A good governess taught a young lady history, geography, and languages; to write in an elegant hand; to draw, sew, and do fancy needlework; to play the pianoforte and possibly the harp; and to carry herself with confidence and elegance. The governess stayed with the family until all the young ladies of the house were married, and sometimes she remained in a family's employ as a companion to the mother or unmarried daughters.

- **Masters.** Visiting masters supplemented a young woman's education with advanced instruction in music, drawing, languages, and dancing. The very best masters were found in the city, but even country neighborhoods usually boasted a few masters who tended to the young ladies in the area.

🌸 **School.** If her parents preferred to not engage a governess, or if a young woman was orphaned or otherwise in need of a settled place to live, a girl might have been sent away to school from age ten to around age eighteen (if she was deemed ready to make her debut in society, she could be withdrawn as much as two years earlier). Schools in London or Bath, often known as young ladies' seminaries, tended to be more formal and fancy. A young lady educated in such an establishment could command an impressive array of accomplishments, including music, drawing, fancy needlework, and a polished and fashionable way of dressing, moving, and behaving. This polish some-times came at the expense of the young lady's health or gave her a falsely inflated sense of self-worth. The luckiest girls were sent to a good old-fashioned board-ing school that provided a less stringent education, but from which they were more likely to emerge healthy and happy and good-natured—such women could always catch up on their education with extensive reading in their fathers' library.

IDENTIFY
"THE QUALITY"

ANNE ELLIOT: *"My idea of good company, Mr. Elliot, is the company of clever, well-informed people, who have a great deal of conversation; that is what I call good company."*
MR. ELLIOT: *"You are mistaken," said he gently, "that is not good company; that is the best. Good company requires only birth, education, and manners, and with regard to education is not very nice."*—PERSUASION

While snobbery of rank should be avoided, everyone knows everyone else's place in the social order. Information on such matters allows one to recognize the most interesting people and enjoyable company. If you are unsure of a particular person's rank, consider the following questions.

◉ **Who is his or her family?** If he or she is related to nobility, then the person in question is most likely a person of breeding and gentility. But even if he or she is related to vulgar persons, it does not immediately follow that he or she is vulgar—the relation may have come through an unwise marriage in the family.

◉ **Does he or she have a title?** Do not expect to meet real aristocracy—that is, lords and ladies—for they mingle only with the very best gentry families. However, one might meet a baronet whose ancestor purchased the title from Charles II or someone who was knighted for making an address to the Crown. One might even meet the grandson of an earl, though one might have to break through barriers of pride and vanity, as well as one's own prejudices, to *truly* know him.

◉ **How long has his or her family lived in one place?** If the family of the individual in question has been living on the same estate for many generations, they are certainly a member of the gentry; however, if the family has little gentility, it might be unpleasant to spend much time in their company. Some members of the family might determine to live and behave in a better way, and an acquaintance with these individuals can be pleasant if one is not overly troubled with the rest of the family.

◉ **Does he or she own an estate or large house, or at least rent one?** Many a fine fortune has been made in trade. This is acceptable once some of the fortune has been converted to land, or at least a good house, allowing the tradesmen to live and entertain properly.

◉ **Does he or she work for a living?** If he or she engages in an acceptable profession, such as the church, the military, or the law, employment is not necessarily a fault; after all, even in the best families, younger sons must be provided for. However, those working in trade or farming land not their own are not the type of people who can expect acceptance among the first families of a place, unless they are particularly genteel or the gentry are particularly liberal in their notions.

◉ **Does he or she live and behave in a genteel manner?** This is probably the most important consideration. Gentility and good breeding can overcome deficiencies of background, and a person might qualify as "good company" in every other respect, but no one wants to spend time with those who have unpleasant manners. Elegance of manner and person, education, and lifestyle can overcome a great deal and admit those who possess them to the very best company indeed.

⚜ **Is he or she rich?** This is not as important as one might think. Money goes a long way, but breeding is more important. Impecunious gentlewomen of good background can be educated, interesting people, as can cash-poor landed gentlemen and younger sons with proper professions. One must be very rich indeed to overcome a suspect background.

FIELD GUIDE TO THE SOCIAL ORDER

Royalty: King George III, Queen Charlotte, and their numerous and dissolute progeny.

Aristocracy: Those entitled to sit in the House of Lords and their families, as well as untitled persons who are very rich, of very old families, or related to peers of the realm. They tend to confine themselves to Georgette Heyer novels and Regency romances, rarely venturing into Jane Austen's settings.

Gentry: Old, established families with estates of all sizes. Nearly all of Jane Austen's characters are drawn from this group. Genteel background is more important than fortune; working in certain professions—the law, the military, or the church—is permissible if one has the proper breeding. Those who have made a fortune in trade and purchased estates can be admitted to this group as long as they give up their shop or warehouse and live in a good sort of way.

Tradesmen and Yeoman Farmers: In many cases indistinguishable from the gentry, except that they work for a living. If they are very rich and genteel, they might mingle with the more enlightened of their betters, but for the most part they keep to themselves to avoid being considered vulgar social climbers.

The Great Unwashed: Laborers, servants, criminals; they rarely appear in Jane Austen's novels except for expositional purposes.

ENSURE A GOOD YEARLY INCOME

*Mr. Darcy soon drew the attention of the room by his
fine, tall person, handsome features, noble mien;
and the report which was in general circulation within
five minutes after his entrance, of his having ten
thousand a year.* —PRIDE AND PREJUDICE

In a society in which one is judged by one's fortune, ensuring
an income that will keep one in the common necessaries of life
is vital. Fortunately, you have a variety of ways in which to
provide for yourself.

Inherit it. A truly grand fortune includes at least one large
estate that provides an ongoing income from rents and the
sale of produce, as well as funded money that produces
interest. Ladies can inherit estates, but they are often
entailed away from the female line (see "Who Died & Made
Mr. Collins the Heir of Longbourn?," page 30). Inheriting
an estate does not ensure a carefree existence, however, as
one must manage it properly and pay it close attention or
one stands in danger of losing it.

Earn it. There are a few genteel professions in which a
gentleman might engage: the church, the military, or the
law (see "Acceptable Men's Professions," page 90). Ladies
are better off employing one of the other methods described
here, as the few professions open to them are poorly paid
(see "How a Lady Might Earn a Living (If Necessary),"
page 87).

MODERN MONEY EQUIVALENTS

While Jane Austen is precise as to the amounts of her characters' personal fortunes, it can be difficult to understand the true value of these fortunes from a distance of two centuries. Some experts suggest simply multiplying the amount by fifty; thus, Mr. Darcy's ten thousand a year becomes a half million pounds, or close to a million dollars.

Economist J. Bradford DeLong of the University of California, Berkeley, suggests that straight multiplication does not give the whole story, and that one must also take into consideration the relative buying power of the amount at that time and place. In those days, goods were expensive and labor cheap, and while a horse might cost as much as 100 pounds, a maidservant's wages for an entire year were less than 10 pounds plus her room and board. Dr. DeLong's calculations place the modern equivalent of Mr. Darcy's income at $6 million per year.

Despite the popular apprehension, Mr. Darcy was not the richest person in Britain, or even close. For example, the Duke of Devonshire's yearly income went to six figures. Some claim that the Duke's house, Chatsworth, was Jane Austen's inspiration for Pemberley, Mr. Darcy's estate. But Mr. Darcy's ten thousand pounds per year could not have supported Chatsworth—though we are certain that Pemberley, however inferior, suited Mr. and Mrs. Darcy perfectly.

◉ **Put your money to work.** Ladies who inherit a cash fortune are wise to put the principal in the Funds and live off the interest, which could be as much as 4 or 5 percent per year. Even gentlemen who have not yet purchased their estate can make an excellent income using this method, and many inheritances include funded money as well as landed estates.

◉ **Marry it.** This is not as easy to do as one might think; one great fortune tends to look out for another great fortune. However, even ladies whose expectations are only one-fifth of four thousand pounds can make matches that will keep them in carriages and pin-money. Some claim that it is a young lady's duty to marry well, but to marry solely for situation or fortune is rarely a good idea unless one's expectations are particularly untoward or one's partner particularly easy to control. However, if the partner in question is not repulsive, marriage is an educated woman's pleasantest preservative from want, and a younger son might find it prudent to supplement his own income by marrying a lady of fortune.

PROVIDE FOR YOUR DAUGHTERS & YOUNGER SONS

Of a very considerable fortune, his son was, by marriage settlements, eventually secure; his present income was an income of independence and comfort. —NORTHANGER ABBEY

If you have married prudently, your eldest son is likely going to inherit an estate, or at least a house and funded money. However, unless you want your other children to be constantly pestering him for money, you must ensure that the younger sons have a means of providing for themselves—and for you and any unmarried daughters should you be left a widow.

◉ **Use your own fortune.** If a lady brings a fortune into her marriage, it is a good idea to have it written into the marriage settlement that her husband is entitled to the income from this money during her lifetime, but that after her death it will be divided among her children. If you are marrying a very rich man, you might even manage to get the income from your fortune strictly for your own use. It's only fair, after all—it's your money! Or your papa's, at least!

◉ **Have your husband settle money upon them.** A lady can insist that her marriage settlement include provisions for her younger children from her husband's fortune. One would not want an overbearing, controlling husband to disinherit children who behaved in a way that did not suit him. And if *you* were given control of their fortune and had

WHO DIED & MADE MR. COLLINS THE HEIR OF LONGBOURN?

Entailments were legal documents created by a family to ensure that an estate would pass down the male line, usually for three generations. The law of primogeniture stated that in the absence of an entailment, the eldest son inherited his father's estate; if he predeceased his father, then the next son would inherit. If there were no sons to inherit the estate, it would be divided among the widow and daughters. Many families used entailments to avoid dividing an estate among several children, partly out of family vanity and partly because partitioning an estate into smaller properties would not provide sufficient income for anyone. An entailment gave residents of the estate only a life interest in its income instead of freehold ownership. If the last generation affected agreed to break the entailment, then the second generation could dispose of pieces of the estate to provide ready cash to defray debt or make dowries for the daughters of the family.

For example, in *Persuasion*, Sir Walter Elliot's estate, Kellynch (and the baronetcy that goes with it), will be inherited by a cousin, William Elliot. Similarly, in *Pride and Prejudice* we are told that Mr. Bennet's estate,

Longbourn, is entailed on the male line; thus, because the Bennets had only daughters, Longbourn will be inherited by a distant cousin, Mr. Collins.

It is unlikely that Mr. Bennet would have voluntarily entered into such an arrangement, so we may assume that he is the second generation of the Longbourn entailment and Mr. Collins is the third. We may further assume that an application to Mr. Collins to break the entailment would not be well received (and imagine what Lady Catherine would have to say about it!). A prudent father would have saved part of his yearly income to provide for his daughters, but Mr. Bennet had depended on having a son to break the entailment and therefore did not save anything.

Most men expected their brides to have a dowry or the expectation of an inheritance, and the six Bennet sisters had only the expectation of dividing their mother's personal fortune of four thousand pounds after her death. The Bennet ladies enjoyed a comfortable lifestyle while Mr. Bennet lived, but they were placed at a disadvantage in the marriage market by having such small expectations. If they remained unmarried when Mr. Bennet died, they would be left without a home and very little money. One might nurture a Jane Bennet-ish hope that Mr. Collins would provide some assistance to the widow and orphans, though probably in vain.

a little tiff with the younkers, one would not wish to be able to cut them off irrevocably; how embarrassing to have to go back on your word later! Clearly, it is better to have these things settled from the beginning.

◉ **If your estate is under entailment, persuade the heir to break it.** If the heir is a grasping sort, there is little chance of succeeding in this endeavor, but it is worth a try. A loving son would, of course, take care of his mama and sisters. (For more on entailments, see "Who Died & Made Mr. Collins the Heir of Longbourn?," page 30.)

◉ **Provide a means for the child to make a living.** If a son is inclined toward the church, send him to one of the universities and set him up in a family living. If he is inclined to the armed services, buy him a commission or find him a naval mentor. If he wants to be a barrister or a physician, arrange for his professional training. If the child is an ingratiating sort and there are rich, childless relatives about, introduce the child in the proper quarters and hope for the best.

◉ **Educate your daughters.** An elegant, accomplished, educated lady will be more likely to contract a brilliant marriage with a man of fortune and breeding. If the worst happens, she will be able to make a living as a governess or a teacher in a school, though of course one hopes one's daughters will never be put to such shifts.

◉ **Put aside some of your yearly income, or assist your husband in doing so, for the benefit of your daughters.** At the very least, your daughters will have some extra cash that might help an eligible gentleman to make up his mind.

RELIGION & THE CHURCH

Like their creator, Jane Austen's characters are members of the Church of England. Jane received her religious instruction from her clergyman father. According to Austen scholar Irene Collins, the Rev. George Austen's opinions on religion were influenced by the theories of the Enlightenment, a philosophic movement that proposed that with proper guidance mankind's innate sense of reason would lead people to do the right thing—a clear departure from the strict, grim Puritanism of previous generations.

While Jane (and her characters) tied morality to religion, she was not tremendously influenced by the two eighteenth-century movements that rose in opposition to Enlightenment philosophies and challenged the Anglican orthodoxy: the Methodists and the Evangelicals. Both of these groups believed in biblical infallibility—that the text and teachings of the Bible are the perfect realization of God's will—and the Evangelicals espoused personal conversion as an essential doctrine. Herself deeply religious, Jane distrusted the Evangelicals' showy display of religion, though later in her life she expressed sympathy for the force of faith behind it.

SPEND EACH SEASON

"What are men to rocks and mountains? Oh! what hours
of transport we shall spend! And when we do return,
it shall not be like other travellers, without being able to
give one accurate idea of any thing. We will know where
we have gone—we will recollect what we have seen."
—ELIZABETH BENNET IN *PRIDE AND PREJUDICE*

Who says that Jane Austen's characters are retired and provincial? They travel from home to Bath to London to the Lake District to country estates and the seaside. The destinations are not arbitrary; they are dictated by means, health, weather, and the location of charming acquaintances. While it is not unknown to go somewhere in the off-season, it is best to know when a place will be unbearably hot, or the company inhumanly thin, so that one might choose the best time for a visit to all the best areas.

LONDON

London is a convenient place to pass through on the way elsewhere, to have unexpected meetings, to do some shopping, to get a picture framed, or to take advantage of the art and culture that only can be experienced in the capital.

BEST TIME TO GO: January through May; "The Season" swings into high gear after Easter.

THINGS TO DO IN LONDON
◉ **Shop.** You will not only have your own shopping to do but that of friends and relatives left behind in the provinces.

London has the best warehouses, and one can purchase material for clothing as well as commission its making-up in the latest fashion. One can purchase books, dishes, furniture, jewelry, music, home decorations—everything that one might want or need.

- **Attend balls and evening parties.** If you are fortunate enough to have acquaintances in London, they will most likely hold evening entertainments with dancing; you may also be invited to the evening parties of their acquaintances. Have a care that you are not seduced by fashionable vices and villains lurking in the big city.

- **Attend the theater.** The theaters at Covent Garden and Drury Lane are the premier venues in the country, where Sarah Siddons, John Kemble, Edmund Kean, and all the best actors can be seen. If your taste runs more to equestrian shows, try Astley's Amphitheatre.

- **Visit museums.** Museums are in abundance in the capital: the National Gallery for paintings, the British Museum for the Elgin Marbles and other antiquities from the far-flung corners of the empire, and Bullock's Museum for natural history.

- **Take advantage of city masters.** The very best instructors in drawing, music, and dancing live in London.

BATH

The city of Bath may not be as popular as it was in years past, but there is no doubt that for those inclined to enjoy city life, Bath offers a variety of activities—and one never knows whom one might meet there!

BEST TIME TO GO: Late autumn, winter, and early spring.

THINGS TO DO IN BATH

◉ **Take the waters.** Those in Bath for their health will drink or bathe in the hot mineral waters of the baths, but even the young and healthy will benefit from drinking a glass each day.

◉ **Promenade at the Pump Room or at the Royal Crescent.** Everyone goes to the Pump Room, ostensibly to drink the waters, but really to see and be seen. If no one worth seeing is in attendance, try strolling along the Royal Crescent for fine views over green fields (and if you're lucky, a fine view of a particular gentleman).

◉ **Shop.** The shops are not as good as those in London, but one can step out of doors and get a thing in five minutes, from clothing to pastry to millinery to the very latest publications.

◉ **Attend the balls.** The Assembly Rooms (Upper and Lower) are open to all who have paid the subscription. There is a regular schedule of balls at each establishment, and a young lady need not fear being without a partner, as the masters of ceremonies stand ready to introduce likely

DID JANE AUSTEN REALLY HATE BATH?

In 1801, Jane Austen left the Hampshire village of Steventon, the home she had known for twenty-five years, and moved to Bath with her parents and her sister. Her father died in 1805, and in 1806 the Austen ladies left Bath, as Jane said later in a letter to Cassandra, "with what happy feelings of escape!" She never returned, though Bath is the setting for a great deal of her last completed novel, *Persuasion*, written in 1816.

It has become an accepted truth among Austen scholars that Jane Austen did not like Bath. The view stems from a few lines in her surviving letters and the portrayal of Bath in *Persuasion* as a stifling place of petty snobberies. Like Jane Austen, *Persuasion*'s Anne Elliot is forced to move from her beloved country home to Bath; like Anne, Jane must have always associated Bath with the death of a parent. Jane wrote little during her years there, which many attribute to her dislike for the place.

However, Jane Austen rarely dealt in extremes. If Jane did not love a place, it does not necessarily follow that she must *hate* it. Perhaps she did not write anything during those years because she was busy with the many activities that life in a town offers, or because she suffered low spirits from the death of her father. There is no doubt, however, that Jane loved the tranquil Hampshire countryside to which she returned in 1808. It was there, in the village of Chawton, that she revised and wrote the six novels that are her legacy.

young men. There are cards and tea for those beyond their dancing days.

◉ **Attend the theater.** The Theatre Royal boasts shows as good as in London; indeed, sometimes even the great actors and actresses are in residence.

◉ **Attend concerts.** There are weekly concerts at the Upper Assembly Rooms on Wednesdays, featuring small instrumental ensembles, singers, or soloists, sometimes sponsored by wealthy patrons. You might hear some beautiful Italian love songs and meet a handsome music lover.

◉ **Attend private parties.** These can be rather boring; nothing but cards and conversation with insipid persons of more consequence than wit. However, with a little contrivance, one might manage to have a tête-à-tête with someone much more interesting.

◉ **Take a country walk.** Bath is a small city, compact and walkable, and it is surrounded by very fine country. One can walk (mostly up very steep hills) to Beechen Cliff for a fine view over the city, explore the country villages in the area surrounding Bath, or just wander through the green and lovely Sydney Gardens.

◉ **Take a ride in an open carriage.** Bristol (and Blaise Castle) is only a short drive away, though one must remember that a clean gown has not five minutes' wear in an open carriage, and young men and women seen riding together in open carriages can be quite a shocking thing.

◉ **Check out the circulating libraries.** A young lady can find works of the most horrid nature there, just fit for a heroine!

THE COUNTRY

BEST TIME TO GO: Summer and autumn, when the cities are unbearable and the sportsmen are in the country. The Christmas season is also pleasantly spent at a country house.

THINGS TO DO IN THE COUNTRY

🌼 **Walk the grounds.** Most grand houses have shrubberies or pleasure grounds or even prettyish little wildernesses to provide exercise for ladies. The more adventurous might roam the countryside, their petticoats six inches deep in mud.

🌼 **Visit friends.** Paying calls is more difficult in the country because of the distances between neighbors, but wheedle the carriage or go on horseback if you must to keep up with the latest gossip and news.

🌼 **Walk into town.** If you are so fortunate as to have a town nearby, it can be an invaluable place to pass time, make purchases, and meet interesting strangers.

🌼 **Produce home theatricals.** A group of friends staying in the same house might decide to act out scenes from a play or perhaps the whole thing. Not only are such theatricals a pleasant way to pass the time, they also provide opportunities for private rehearsals, possibly with the object of your interest. Do not listen to do-gooders who try to persuade you that such activities are improper.

◉ **Read the books you bought in the city.** Long, rainy days or boring evenings are best passed with the latest publications, whether novels such as *The Mysteries of Udolpho* by Anne Radcliffe, an epic poem such as *Marmion* by Walter Scott, or books of information such as Boswell's *Life of Johnson* or Goldsmith's *An History of the Earth*.

◉ **Attend neighborhood balls.** Unless circumstances are particularly untoward, you may expect your neighbors to hold a series of balls, especially during the full moon when traveling at night is easier. If a neighbor needs encouragement, do not be afraid to tease him into having a ball.

◉ **Tour fine houses richly furnished.** Country hospitality allows travelers to drop in and request a tour of any grand estate. The housekeeper will most likely know the house better than the owners and will be pleased to show you around. Give her a tip for her trouble.

◉ **Improve your estate.** Build a hermitage or a Grecian temple, root up all the trees in the avenue, tear down unsightly cottages, add shrubbery or a gravel walk, replace an old casement window with a larger bow window to improve the view from the house—with a little imagination, every house can be improved!

THE SEASIDE

BEST TIME TO GO: Summer is high season, though the southern coast has a relatively mild climate year round; some have been known to bathe in the sea as late in the year as November.

THINGS TO DO AT THE SEASIDE

◉ **Bathe.** Most seaside resorts have bathing machines, like little wooden huts on wheels. One enters on the beach side and changes into a flannel shift for bathing as the machine is rolled into the sea. Open the door on the seaside and the attendant will "dip" you into the waves. In moderation, this is a beneficial activity, but be careful not to tire yourself.

◉ **Shop.** The best resorts have very good shops, but do not expect much in the way of selection.

◉ **Walk on the beach.** Walking is excellent exercise, and the salt air is beneficial for those suffering from weaknesses of the lungs.

◉ **Promenade on the Cobb or the Marine Parade.** Tie the strings of your bonnet tightly so it is not carried away by the ocean breeze.

How to
WRITE A LETTER

HENRY TILNEY: *"As far as I have had opportunity of judging, it appears to me that the usual style of letter-writing among women is faultless, except in three particulars."*
CATHERINE MORLAND: *"And what are they?"*
HENRY: *"A general deficiency of subject, a total inattention to stops, and a very frequent ignorance of grammar."*
—*NORTHANGER ABBEY*

The recipient of a letter must pay for its postage based on the weight of the letter and how far it traveled. It is rude to expect someone to pay for extra pages, so confine yourself to one sheet or two at the most. Clever letter writers can keep their letters to one page while still cramming them full of the latest news and gossip.

1. **Start with a large sheet of paper.** Write the date and your current address at the top of the sheet.

2. **Write neatly on one side of the sheet.**

3. **When the sheet is filled, turn the paper 180 degrees.** Continue to write, upside-down, between the lines you wrote previously.

4. **Turn the paper 90 degrees in either direction.** Continue writing at a right angle across the lines you have already written *(Fig. A)*.

5. **Fold the paper into its own envelope.** With the blank side

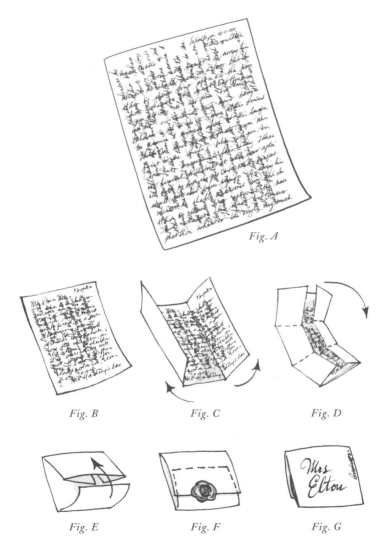

Fig. A

Fig. B

Fig. C

Fig. D

Fig. E

Fig. F

Fig. G

underneath *(Fig. B)*, fold in each long side to meet in the middle *(Fig. C)*. (If you have more to say, you can write on the blank flaps as well, but they might be visible to anyone who handles the letter.) Fold the letter up on itself into three or four sections, leaving a little room between the top edge and the uppermost fold *(Fig. D)*. Tuck the bottom flap into the sides of the top flap to make a little package *(Fig. E)*.

6. **Seal the letter.** Heat a stick of wax over a candle and place a few drops on the flap, pressing down with an embossed seal for a pretty touch *(Fig. F)*. If you find that method too messy, use a wafer made of flour and gum backed with paper. The waxy side becomes sticky when moistened and makes an excellent seal that will not melt in hot weather.

7. **Direct the letter.** On the unsealed side, write out the direction (address)—the person's name (the eldest unmarried daughter's address is simply Miss Bennet; younger daughters are addressed as Miss Elizabeth Bennet), village, and county *(Fig. G)*. If the address is in London, add the street address, as letters are delivered to one's house there; in the country one must pick up one's letters at the village post office. If your letter is being franked (see "Franking," opposite), leave it blank in case the person doing the franking is particular about directing it himself.

8. **Deliver the letter to the post office.** Have a servant run the errand, or do it yourself if this is a private communication.

NOTE: For invitations and other short notes that will be hand-carried by a servant, an elegant little sheet of hot-pressed paper will serve nicely; simply wrap it in a plain sheet of the same paper and seal it.

HOW TO BE A GOOD CORRESPONDENT

◉ **Add extra pages if it will not increase the recipient's cost.** If a kind neighbor offers to carry a letter to a distant friend, take him up on it, because then you can write as much as you like.

◉ **Always write when news is expected, whether it is good or bad.** It is unkind to leave friends in suspense, and when they have no news to impart to the neighborhood, the neighborhood may make up unkind news to fill the void.

◉ **Send a half crown under the seal.** This will help the recipient defray the cost of postage when a letter is not franked.

◉ **Have a care with the direction.** You would not want your friends to miss important news. Even if you are upset, take the time to write carefully!

FRANKING

If you were so fortunate as to have a member of either house of Parliament handy, he could "frank" your letters so the recipient would not have to pay for postage. The person franking the letter was supposed to sign the front of the letter in addition to writing the recipient's name and direction, but in many cases he simply signed his name to a letter that already had been directed.

◉ **Write bad news only when it is definite.** Do not make conjectures that will alarm your family with premature apprehension.

◉ **Speak of more than just money.** Do not make an application for financial assistance the obvious point of the letter. Ask after the folks back home, and tell them a little bit about what's going on in your life.

◉ **Bear in mind the consequences of your words.** Do not write anything unflattering about someone you may want to impress later—such letters can be saved and produced at inconvenient times.

◉ **Do not end a courtship via letter.** No one ever looks good doing so.

OF BILLETS-DOUX

It was exceedingly improper for unmarried, unrelated persons of the opposite sex to correspond. Nonetheless, there are examples of such correspondence in almost all of Jane Austen's novels.

- In *Sense and Sensibility*, Marianne Dashwood wrote several letters to Willoughby, and her acquaintances therefore assumed they were engaged. Even Elinor, whom one would expect to know her sister's secrets, began to think so.

- *Pride and Prejudice*'s Mr. Darcy writes a letter to Elizabeth Bennet to correct her misapprehensions about him. He seeks her out at a time when he knows she will be alone and hands her the letter, though he is uncomfortable seeing her, rather than sending a servant who might spread gossip.

- Edmund Bertram writes to Fanny Price in *Mansfield Park*, but she is his *cousin*, and he is in love with Mary Crawford at the time in any event.

- Jane Austen hints that *Northanger Abbey*'s Henry Tilney and Catherine Morland exchanged letters while they waited for General Tilney to change his mind about giving his blessing to their marriage. Catherine's parents "looked the other way" because they knew that Henry and Catherine considered themselves as good as engaged and trusted that the general would change his mind eventually.

- In *Persuasion*, Captain Wentworth pours out his heart to Anne Elliot in a letter, which he cannot hand to her openly, but with true naval fervor he finds a way to get it to her nonetheless.

GET AROUND

"Well, my dear," said Mrs. Jennings, "and how did you travel?"
"Not in the stage, I assure you," replied Miss Steele, with quick
exultation; "we came post all the way, and had a very smart
beau to attend us. Dr. Davies was coming to town, and so we
thought we'd join him in a post-chaise; and he behaved very
genteelly, and paid ten or twelve shillings more than we did."
—SENSE AND SENSIBILITY

Getting from place to place is fraught with anxiety for ladies,
since motorized transportation won't be an option until the
twentieth century. Travel over long distances requires horse-
power—literally. The level of comfort provided in the travel
accommodations is determined by the amount a person can
pay. Here's a rundown of your options for moving about the
country, in journeys short and long.

SHORT DISTANCES

❀ **Walk.** If you are so fortunate as to live near a village that
boasts shops and neighbors to visit, take advantage of your
situation. The exercise will bring a glow to your complexion
and a sparkle to your eyes that gentlemen will notice far
more than the mud on your petticoat.

❀ **Ride on horseback.** If walking is too fatiguing, horseback
riding is excellent exercise and will get you out in the fresh
air without overtiring you. (See "How to Ride Sidesaddle,"
page 52.)

Hire a sedan chair. The chair consists of a closed box with a seat, an opening in the front, and poles along each side. Two chairmen use the poles to  carry the chair through city streets. Sedan chairs are very popular in Bath because of the confluence of elderly and ill people, steep hills, and the expense and difficulty of maintaining one's own carriage. Even the young and healthy use them to get home from evening engagements. They are not unknown in London but are rarely seen in the country.

Drive a donkey cart. If your personal situation does not permit keeping a carriage, a donkey cart—a plain wooden cart drawn by a single donkey—is ideal for travel in good weather in the country, especially for older ladies. Donkeys are easier to control than horses and cheaper to maintain; just hope that the stubborn little beast doesn't stand in the middle of the road and refuse to move.

Join a gentleman in an open carriage. Young men sometimes drive sporty, fast-moving, two-wheeled open carriages drawn by one horse  (called a gig) or two (called a curricle). Taking a ride can lead to a pleasant afternoon in the country, but as these vehicles only seat two, you will need another couple in a second equipage to travel with you or you risk having your reputation compromised. Bear in mind that a clean gown quickly soils on the dusty roads, and if it rains, you will be soaked.

Travel by private carriage. Whether the carriage is a four-wheeled phaeton suitable for a woman to drive or a six-seated barouche with a driver, private carriages offer the ideal method for traveling in all cases. Keeping one's own carriage is an expensive proposition, as horse feed and stabling is costly, but any family with pretensions to gentility will keep their own carriage and two to four horses to pull it.

Hire a hack. A carriage and horses can be hired from the local livery stable to transport one to a particular event, such as a ball. However, this is a poor substitute for having your own carriage, as it will give your neighbors an excuse to patronize you.

LONGER DISTANCES

Hire a post-chaise. A four-wheeled closed carriage drawn by two to four horses is the fastest, easiest, and most comfortable method of traveling long distances—and the most expensive. The cost depends upon the distance traveled. The chaise will stop regularly to change horses, so you will not be delayed while the horses are fed and watered. While traveling, young ladies should be accompanied by a family member or a servant; a maidservant may ride inside, or a manservant can ride beside the chaise. If a young lady is going home from a country house, she should be offered the escort of a manservant for part of her journey, and it is to be hoped that her parents will send their own servant to meet her and escort her the rest of the way. To expect a well-bred young girl to travel alone is a serious breach of propriety.

⚜ **Journey by private carriage.** Long-distance travel in one's own carriage offers the benefit of setting the schedule, the comfort of one's own vehicle, and the confidence inspired by one's own driver. However, long distances using one's own horses can be slower than hiring a post-chaise, as the horses will need to stop regularly to rest. One might rent a set of fresh horses for the next leg of the trip and send back a groom to return them and fetch your own horses, but doing so creates additional expense and annoyance.

⚜ **Catch a ride with the mail.** For a small fee, one might ride along on a Royal Mail coach, as long as one is traveling on a scheduled route. This is a good way to travel between large cities, but might have to be combined with a post-chaise to reach far-flung destinations. Young ladies should not ride on the mail coach unescorted.

⚜ **Travel by stagecoach.** This is the cheapest and slowest way to travel. On a stagecoach one will pay for the privilege of an interminably slow ride on a nobleman's castoff conveyance, crammed next to all the ragtag and bobtail of the kingdom. Avoid this type of travel except as an absolute last resort, and never take the trip unaccompanied!

RIDE SIDESADDLE

"It is a pleasure to see a lady with such a good heart for riding!" said he. "I never see one sit a horse better. She did not seem to have a thought of fear. Very different from you, miss, when you first began, six years ago come next Easter. Lord bless you! how you did tremble when Sir Thomas first had you put on!" —COACHMAN IN *MANSFIELD PARK*

Ladies ride sidesaddle not only because riding astride in a gown would be scandalous, but because it is safer, especially for petite women. If you are not very athletic and do not have strong legs, it is quite difficult to hang onto a horse while riding astride. Proper use of the sidesaddle will enable you to stay safely on the horse's back and enjoy riding even at a fast trot. Before starting, be sure you are dressed properly (see "How to Dress," page 000) and that your horse is trained for sidesaddle riding.

1. **Saddle the horse.** Ask the groom to strap the saddle on your horse. Check that it is snugly fastened and that the bridle is properly buckled. The bit should rest comfortably in the horse's mouth.

2. **Approach the mounting block.** The groom will lead the horse to the mounting block, or he or a gentleman friend with whom you are riding will lace his fingers together to give you a step up. Do not attempt to mount the horse from the ground, as it will be both immodest and exceedingly undignified. Lead the horse to a fence or large rock if you are out in a field with no one around—but a well-bred young lady would *never* find herself in such a position.

3. **Mount the horse.** Hold the pommel of the saddle with your right hand and place your left hand on the shoulder of your gentleman friend. Place your left foot in the stirrup. Your gentleman friend will then place his hands on your waist. Press on his shoulder as he lifts you into the saddle.

4. **Position yourself in the saddle.** Set your right leg into the U-shaped horn, which should rest just above your knee. Then sit up straight, facing forward, with your weight on your right leg and your hips and shoulders square with the horse's head.

5. **Indicate the proper length as your gentleman friend adjusts the stirrup.** If you are feeling daring, pull up your skirt a bit and give him a flash of ankle as he does so. Do not flash your ankle if the groom is performing this service! When he is finished, arrange your skirt, which might be slightly longer and fuller on the left side to modestly cover your legs and feet.

6. **Take up the reins.** Place one in each hand, weaving them under your little finger, over the next two fingers, and under your forefinger. Hold your riding crop loosely in your right hand, angled back to touch the horse's side.

7. **Pull back *gently* on the reins.** Do not yank them or you will hurt and annoy the horse. The horse will pull forward on the bit, gently if she is well-trained. Once you have established contact, loosen the reins a bit.

8. **Communicate to the horse with signals.** To get the horse to walk, press your left leg against the horse's side while pressing into its right side with your crop, substituting the feel of a rider's right leg. To speed into a trot, loosen the reins a bit

and press once more with your left leg and crop. To stop the horse, pull back gently on the reins, press the horse's sides with your left leg and your crop, and press down with your backside. Very well-trained horses might respond to verbal commands such as a tongue click. Do not go faster than a trot or jump the horse until you have a great deal of experience. Only the fast girls follow the hounds, anyway.

SECTION II:

A Quick Succession of Busy Nothings; or, Everyday Activities

How to
KEEP HOUSE

"Catherine would make a sad, heedless young house-keeper to be sure," was her mother's foreboding remark; but quick was the consolation of there being nothing like practice. —**NORTHANGER ABBEY**

The mistress of a house is rather like the CEO of a major cor-poration. She oversees all operations: food service, personnel, training, procurement, budget, charitable contributions, inte-rior design, and the day-to-day household activities. There are some ladies who delegate decision-making (and virtually all active involvement) to their housekeeper or a grown-up daughter, but one cannot imagine any of Jane Austen's hero-ines doing so after their marriages. No doubt they would plan menus themselves and ensure that their children were cared for and educated, their husbands comfortable and well-fed, and their budget well in hand, all with a smile and a metaphorical The Buck Stops Here sign on their elegant Sheraton writing desks.

◉ **Develop a good relationship with your housekeeper.** It is likely that she came with the house, has been with the family for ages, and changed your husband's diapers, so do not dismiss her out of hand. Tap into her institutional wisdom and follow her suggestions whenever practicable, but never let her forget that you are the mistress and she is the servant. It is best to make her your ally and not your enemy, for she can make you look like a superstar—or a slattern.

◉ Work with your cook. Help him or her to plan menus and purchase food for daily meals and dinner parties. Take care to stay within your budget on food. Large dinners for just the family are wasteful, especially since there is no dependable method of preserving food. Your husband will be satisfied with one well-prepared course for his dinner—save your big guns for dinner parties.

◉ Oversee the servants. Much of the daily interaction with the servants can be delegated to your housekeeper, but at the least you should know the name and function of each person working in your house (see "Servants, By Duty & Rank," page 62).

◉ Look after your less fortunate neighbors. There might be a perfectly genteel family—the widow or unmarried daughter of your late vicar, for instance—who is having difficulty making ends meet. Do not insult them by offering them money, though they will welcome an occasional gift of a hindquarter of pork or bushel of apples. Pay a personal visit every week or two, even if their company is a trifle tiresome.

◉ Take care of the poor and sick. Visit them, deliver food, give advice, listen to their complaints. It is not fun, but it is your duty. The indigent have no other support system (and your visits offer a good way to get rid of leftovers).

◉ Improve your interiors. It is likely that your house is filled with heavy, gloomy furniture, dark paneling, and other old-fashioned, vulgar stuff inherited from previous generations. Refurnish your rooms with light, elegant furniture and colors. You live in a time of elegant style; take advantage of it!

⚜ **Look after the family sewing.** Your dressmaker and your husband's tailor will make most of the new clothing for the family, but repairs and some basic sewing are the responsibility of the lady of the house and any daughters old enough to assist. Do not forget the poor; ensure that new babies have clothes and that the poor are decently clad. Gifts of old gowns and new underwear are always appreciated.

⚜ **Teach your children.** If they are too young for a governess, you can teach them their letters and numbers yourself. As your daughters get older, it is your responsibility to oversee their education: hire masters, ensure that they are acquiring the accomplishments that their husbands will expect, and train them to run their own houses. You do not want a bunch of spinsters left on your hands, do you?

THE MASTER'S RESPONSIBILITIES

If the mistress of a great house is its CEO, then the master is the CFO and physical plant manager. An estate owner might gain his riches from the sweat of his tenants, but in turn he makes sure they are clothed, fed, and housed. Jane Austen's heroes take this charge seriously: If the crops fail, everyone suffers.

⚜ **Oversee agricultural activity.** The landowner usually has a bailiff to whom many of the daily tasks are designated, but a wise landowner will keep his hand in, riding out to inspect the crops or herds and conferring with his tenants firsthand.

⚜ **Improve the estate.** This can involve anything from landscaping to constructing greenhouses or even overseeing the design and construction of a whole new house.

◉ **Participate in local government.** In many cases, the master of an estate is also the local magistrate, responsible for tending to criminal matters and sorting out disagreements among the locals. He might be a churchwarden as well, requiring him to maintain the parish church and ensure that the rector receives the tithes to which he is entitled.

◉ **Maintain an open-door policy.** The tenants, especially the younger men, often approach the estate owner with questions and problems about their crops, livestock, and love life. Listen to them and give advice and guidance.

◉ **Provide social security.** Ensure that everyone dependent on your estate has adequate shelter and enough to eat; however, don't let the lazy bums take advantage of your good nature. Be compassionate, but prod tenants to action when necessary.

SERVANTS, BY DUTY & RANK

There were no labor-saving appliances in Jane Austen's time, but human labor could be purchased cheaply. In *Emma*, even the Bateses, who were grateful for gifts of produce from more well-to-do neighbors, had a maidservant, Patty. Large estates had a bewildering retinue of servants to tend to one's every need.

Bailiff: Acted as middle manager between the master and the laborers regarding the estate's agricultural concerns.

Steward: Dealt with household administrative issues, hired and fired domestic staff, paid bills, and assisted with the master's correspondence. Stewards were sometimes also responsible for the bailiff's duties. In smaller establishments without a steward, the butler performed some of these duties.

Butler: Answered the door and admitted callers, supervised the footmen, lit and extinguished candles, tended to the fires, oversaw the polishing of the silver service, and cared for the wine cellar.

Housekeeper: Supervised the maids, oversaw housecleaning and laundry, and liaised between the mistress and the cook.

Cook: Supervised the kitchen, including dishwashing and meal preparation.

Valet: Cared for his master's clothing and personal needs. Did not mingle with the other servants.

Lady's Maid: Cared for the mistress's clothing, occasionally sewing them herself or making gowns over to reflect changing fashions; looked after her jewelry; and styled her hair. She kept for her own use any clothes her mistress no longer wanted.

Governess: Taught and cared for older children. Did not associate with the lower servants.

Footmen: Served at dinner, fetched things, conveyed messages, carried purchases home from the shops, delivered their mistress's calling cards, and generally made themselves useful. Usually chosen for their good looks.

Nursemaid: Fed, dressed, and played with the children who were too young for a governess, generally keeping them out of their parents' way.

Housemaids: Cleaned and tidied public areas of the house, under the housekeeper's supervision. Chosen for their youth and beauty.

Coachman, Grooms, Stable Boys: Drove and maintained the carriages and cared for the horses.

Gardeners: Tended to landscaping. Some large houses had a head gardener and underlings.

Scullery Maids: Washed dishes and performed difficult scrubbing and cleaning tasks. Usually very young girls or women deemed too unattractive to be housemaids.

Manservant: Executed heavy lifting; cleaned up after cows; and other messy tasks in households insufficiently grand to have footmen.

Washerwoman: Generally not on staff; came from the village as needed and either did the laundry on-site or took it to her home.

PLAN A DINNER PARTY

"I think every thing has passed off uncommonly well, I assure you. The dinner was as well dressed as any I ever saw. The venison was roasted to a turn—and everybody said they never saw so fat a haunch. The soup was fifty times better than what we had at the Lucases' last week; and even Mr. Darcy acknowledged, that the partridges were remarkably well done; and I suppose he has two or three French cooks at least."

—MRS. BENNET IN *PRIDE AND PREJUDICE*

Giving a dinner party (see "How to Behave at a Dinner Party," page 142) is fraught with drama for any hostess. Good employees and a solid plan are the keys to success.

1. **Consult with your housekeeper.** She will have all the information you need at her fingertips: the condition of the household linens, the state of the pantry, and any problems with staffing levels that might interfere with the smooth running of your event.

2. **Plan your menu.** Consider what is available in the current season and what kind of food can be obtained locally, and choose your dishes accordingly.

3. **Plan your guest list.** Keep in mind the temper of your guests. If there is someone who does not like large dinner parties, he might make the party unpleasant.

4. **Write out your invitations.** Inscribe each note individually, tailoring each to the recipient.

5. **Speak with your cook.** Finalize the menu; be sure to serve the favorite dishes of your most prominent guests, especially potential suitors to any of your daughters.

6. **Have your husband discuss the wine list with the butler.** Give them the menu and let them handle it. It's one less detail you will have to concern yourself with.

7. **Prepare to meet your guests' special needs.** If you have invited someone who is an invalid, be sure that you have a special screen for the fire; if there is a drafty area, be sure the young ladies will have shawls to wrap themselves up.

SCHEDULE OF MEALS

Breakfast. *Around 10 A.M.* A light meal of toast and bread served with tea, coffee, or perhaps chocolate (a bitter brew more like liquefied dark chocolate than the creamy, sweet beverage to which modern palates are accustomed). Grand houses might provide cake and rolls and even cold meat left over from the previous day's dinner. Older gentlemen might expect the heartier breakfast of their youth: A fried chop and a mug of ale.

Luncheon/Nuncheon. *Midday.* Not a formal meal; if one is peckish in the middle of the day, a snack of cold meat and bread and butter might be wheedled from the cook. One also might expect to be served tea and cake or perhaps even fruit, cold meat, or sandwiches while paying a morning call.

Dinner. *3–5 P.M. in the country; 6–7 P.M. or later if following "town hours" in very fashionable households.*

Tea. *An hour after dinner.* This is not the formal meal it became in Victorian times. One might be invited to a house not to dine but only to "drink tea," which means arriving after dinner for tea, coffee, and perhaps cake.

Supper. *9–10 P.M. if dinner is early; if dinner is fashionably late, it might be dispensed with entirely.* Supper can be a hot sit-down meal or a light snack of English muffins, toast and butter, tea and coffee, and perhaps a bit of wine mixed with water as a digestive and sleep aid. Valetudinarians such as Mr. Woodhouse will accept nothing more than a bowl of nice thin gruel.

IMPROVE YOUR ESTATE

"Had I a place to new fashion, I should not put myself into the hands of an improver, I would rather have an inferior degree of beauty, of my own choice, and acquired progressively. I would rather abide by my own blunder than by his."
—EDMUND BERTRAM IN *MANSFIELD PARK*

So the old man has finally been gathered to his fathers and the estate is yours at last! For so long you have looked at his manicured, regulated gardens and gloomy interiors and dreamed of the showplace the family pile could be. Assuming you have the funds, here is how you can go about creating it.

1. **Find the perfect situation for the house.** If the current house is in a low spot where no one can see it properly, build a new house on rising ground, or reshape the existing grounds to better show off the house and give a good prospect from inside.

2. **Fix the landscaping to highlight natural beauty.** Root up straight avenues of ancient trees and sell them off—the price of the timber will pay for the improvements, and the tree removal will open up the view from the house. Flower gardens should appear as though flowers have sprung up naturally here and there, spilling out into the gravel walkways rather than laid out symmetrically or in straight lines.

3. **Add useless but pretty outbuildings.** An Ionic or Doric temple is just the thing for private assignations, or go all out and build a tiny castle—people will come from miles around to see it.

4. **Add rustic touches.** A hermitage is lovely—recruit an actual hermit to live in it for full realism. Add some ruins, a gravel walk, large rocks covered with moss, and shrubbery for private conversations or even just a shady walk on a hot day. Let sheep roam wild, preferably in groups of three or five, with a sunken fence if you'd prefer to keep them in one area without ruining the view.

5. **Use water to good advantage.** If you are so fortunate as to have a stream on your property, redirect it to cross the front lawn for the most picturesque effect. Perhaps some of it can be dammed up to make a pond or lake, which can be stocked with fish.

6. **Change the look of the house.** Add a new neoclassical wing to the house, or at least a new façade, with columns, domes, and windows. An Eastern influence is also quite fashionable.

THE "PICTURESQUE"

In the mid-eighteenth century, William Gilpin, a clergyman and amateur artist, published several travel journals that incorporated his ideas on picturesque landscape and paintings depicting it. In contrast to the common wisdom of the time, in which gardens were manicured into evenly-shaped beds, he felt a natural state was best, with no straight lines and a rough, rustic feel—a blasted tree, a moss-covered rock, a ruined castle, or other such gloomy items were desirable, arranged in the foreground, middle ground, and distance. If sheep or cows were to be part of a painting, they should be in unevenly numbered groups, with three considered particularly picturesque. If these characteristics did not actually appear in the landscape in front of the artist, it was perfectly acceptable for the artist to insert them.

Gilpin's wildly natural aesthetic worked its way into architecture and landscape design as well as the literature of the time. A Gothic novel, such as *The Mysteries of Udolpho*, would always include a mysterious castle or abbey on the verge of ruin, as well as lengthy poetical descriptions of the rugged mountain country in which it was inevitably located.

RAISE YOUR CHILDREN

"You know it is very bad to have children with one that one is obliged to be checking every moment; 'don't do this,' and 'don't do that;' or that one can only keep in tolerable order by more cake than is good for them."
—MRS. MUSGROVE IN *PERSUASION*

Between a patriarchal social structure and the lack of effective birth control methods, Regency women are almost certain to bear children after marriage, sometimes many children close together. Ideally, both parents would be involved in raising the children, but most of the responsibility falls to the woman. If there is anything disagreeable going on, men are always sure to get out of it!

❧ **Employ your servants to best advantage.** You have hired a trustworthy nurse; let her assist you. Wean the infant after three months and turn it over to her so you can attend to your other duties.

❧ **Keep them in the country as much as possible.** Children need room to run about and play, and in fine weather fresh air is good for a child.

Employ the latest educational methods. Read Jean-Jacques Rousseau's novel *Émile* and John Locke's book *Some Thoughts on Education* for advice. Children are naturally good, and their spirits should be allowed to develop naturally and not repressed.

Instill good principles. Teach them pride in their position in society, but teach them the duties that come with it: caring for those less fortunate and maintaining the family property for the next generation.

Encourage their creativity. Give them books to read, paper upon which to draw, and blank books in which to write stories.

Do not allow them to be idle. Keep them busy, even with play or active pursuits, for idleness leads to ignorance. Do not force a child to apply herself to a subject she does not wish to study, such as music lessons—find another activity to take its place.

Give them treats. If all else fails, liberal slices of cake solve many child-rearing problems.

BECOME KNOWN AS A VALUABLE NEIGHBOR

*"I think there are few places with such society as Highbury.
I always say, we are quite blessed in our neighbours."*
—MISS BATES IN *EMMA*

In the country, it is important to maintain good relations with your neighbors.

◉ **Look after the poor and sick.** Ensure that they have enough food and warm clothing. Give them advice and provide a good example.

◉ **Assist young people with vocational matters.** Use your connections to find a place for a young person in need of a position as a governess or maidservant. If the young person refuses your help, accept her decision gracefully; surely she has a good reason for it.

◉ **Use your resources to spare others trouble.** Offer your carriage to ladies in need of a ride on the night of a ball or dinner party. If you are passing by a neighbor's house, stop and inquire if you can perform any service for them, especially if they are housebound. If you will be traveling and a neighbor has a friend in the area, offer to carry a letter or package to save postage costs.

◉ **Do not gossip about your neighbors.** When they are having family troubles, keeping silent on the matter is probably the best thing you can do for them.

⚜ **Remind others to look after their health.** Teach the young ladies under your purview that a little daily exercise and efforts to help the poor will serve them better than putting on sickly airs and lying about on sofas.

⚜ **Play Cupid.** Invite the young people of the neighborhood over for an evening of card games and a bit of hot supper. If you are going to town for a time, take a young neighbor with you and make sure she gets to the assemblies to meet young men.

⚜ **Give good advice where it is needed.** If a young neighbor is prepared to throw herself away on a half-pay officer or someone equally undesirable, impress upon her the foolishness of such behavior and how she will regret disobliging her family.

TREAT THE SICK

*"We have entirely done with the whole Medical Tribe.
We have consulted Physician after Physician in vain, till
we are quite convinced that they can do nothing for us &
that we must trust to our own knowledge of our own
wretched Constitutions for any relief."*
—DIANA PARKER IN *SANDITON*

In the Regency, medical practitioners believe diseases are caused by an imbalance in the body's four humors (blood, black bile, yellow bile, and phlegm). Obtaining relief or curing disease is simply a matter of determining which humor is in excess and relieving the imbalance through one of the following methods.

- **Bleeding.** Releasing an excess of blood is an excellent treatment for fevers and headaches. Leeches can be purchased at the apothecary; simply attach a leech to the affected area and remove it once it is swollen. One might forgo the leeches and cut open the patient's vein instead, allowing blood to flow until the patient swoons for best effect.

- **Laxatives and emetics.** An excess of bile can be treated with various plants and tinctures that help to purge the body. Better out than in!

- **Taking the water.** The warm, mineral-laden waters that gush from springs in Bath, Cheltenham, and other spa towns act as a laxative, purging one's system of excess bile while the minerals replenish the body. If one is unable to walk to the pump room, one can engage a sedan chair to carry one there. For some maladies, bathing in the water is more effective than drinking it.

◉ **Laudanum.** Tincture of opium can help to relieve pain or calm a nervous complaint. Slip a little into a colicky baby's milk; put a drop or two into your tea if your nerves (or children) are plaguing you; put in a few drops more if you are in real pain.

◉ **Amputation.** When wounds become septic, as they so often do, there is nothing else to be done but to remove the limb. One sees this often in military and naval men; in the heat of battle, surgeons overwhelmed with wounded do not have time for more delicate treatments.

OF MEDICAL MEN

During the Regency period, there were three types of medical men to consult if one was not feeling at all the thing.

Physician: As a gentleman, he was unable to touch the patient or do anything active on the patient's behalf—gentlemen, after all, did not work. Physicians were educated at one of the universities and then attended medical school or trained with another physician.

Surgeon: Surgeons generally had no university degree but trained by dissecting corpses obtained from a "resurrection man" (grave robber) or from the gallows. They set bones, performed amputations, and treated other traumatic injuries but were never to be considered gentlemen.

Apothecary: Apothecaries dispensed drugs prescribed by a physician; some people preferred to cut out the middleman and consulted their apothecary directly for advice on diet and medicine. In country villages, the apothecary was often the only local source of medical advice.

HYPOCHONDRIACS IN JANE AUSTEN'S NOVELS

Mary Musgrove in *Persuasion*: Queen Whiner of the Austen oeuvre, Mary complains of illness mostly in a desperate bid for attention from her husband and in-laws. Mary's sore throats, you know, are always worse than anybody's!

Mrs. Churchill in *Emma*: It is hard to tell if Mrs. Churchill was really ill or just seeking attention, but she certainly used her ailments to keep her nephew Frank dancing in attendance. She was probably as astonished as anyone else when she actually died.

Mrs. Bennet in *Pride and Prejudice*: Mrs. Bennet constantly complains about her "nerves" and takes to her bed when Lydia runs away with Wickham, though her immediate recovery upon word of Lydia's impending marriage renders her initial indisposition suspicious.

Anne deBourgh in *Pride and Prejudice*: Anne is described as "thin and sickly," but one wonders if she (or her overbearing mother) uses her unspecified illnesses to give her an excuse to be average.

Diana, Susan, and Arthur Parker in *Sanditon*: The portrayal of the three hypochondriac Parker siblings is some of the most savagely funny satire in any Austen novel and is especially compelling when one realizes that Jane Austen wrote it as she was suffering from the illness that would kill her only a few months later.

LADY MIGHT SPEND HER LEISURE TIME

It was a quick succession of busy nothings. —MANSFIELD PARK

Though the mistress of a house has many duties to keep her busy, she will have some time to herself. Before her marriage, she spent her free time acquiring accomplishments (see "How to Become an Accomplished Lady," page 16), and while some women prefer to follow other pursuits after their marriage, those who take pleasure in their accomplishments will want to keep up their skills or spend their free time in useful employment.

🌸 **Music.** Constant practice is necessary if one is to excel; two hours a day at one's instrument is optimal. Most genteel families have a pianoforte in their house, so if you concentrate on that instrument you will be able to perform for others most frequently. You may have to invite others to your home to hear you play upon the harp, unless you plan to cart it with you in the carriage. If you wish to play for a particular gentleman, invite him to your home, sit by the French doors, and play. He will love it! Once you are married, of course, you may be tempted to ignore your music entirely, but continued practice will provide you with a worthwhile distraction from the day-to-day.

🌸 **Drawing.** Pencil sketches, filled in with watercolors, are a ladylike accomplishment and produce lovely items to hang in one's drawing room or sitting room. If one has a taste for the picturesque, one's productions can be truly artistic!

◉ **Reading.** Make up a list of serious books, such as James Fordyce's *Sermons to Young Women* or Vicesimus Knox's *Elegant Extracts in Prose*, and work your way through it. If you must read novels, be sure they are the improving sort, with proper heroines who listen to their parents and rarely make bad decisions, such as *Pamela* by Samuel Richardson or *Evelina* by Fanny Burney. Ann Radcliffe's Gothic novels, such as *The Mysteries of Udolpho* and *The Romance of the Forest*, have heroines of superior habits and understanding and are less objectionable than other novels of that sort.

◉ **Fancy needlework.** If you can put off most of the plain sewing on your servants and your daughters, you will have time for fancy work, such as:

• *Embroidery.* Trace a pattern lightly onto your fabric with a pencil and stitch over it, then wash out the pencil marks. White embroidery on white muslin is beautiful; embroider a gown or a shawl with running stitch *(Fig. A)* and satin stitch *(Fig. B)* and wait for the compliments to roll in!

• *Carpet work.* Use wool yarn to stitch a tapestry carpet on canvas. Use it to cover a footstool or a chair seat.

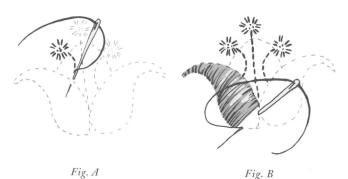

Fig. A   Fig. B

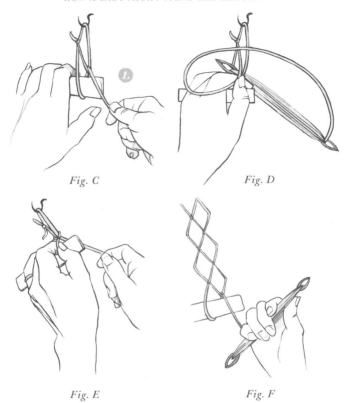

Fig. C

Fig. D

Fig. E

Fig. F

- *Netting.* Make yourself a purse or a sweet cloak by winding worsted yarn or cotton or silk thread onto a netting needle and tying knots to form a mesh fabric *(Figs. C–F)*. Use a wooden or bone gauge to keep the mesh even *(Fig. C-1)*. Knots can be tied in patterns, or if you are making a fine mesh, you can embroider over it later to create filet lace. If you have a sailor around the house, he will know this skill, which is used to make fishing nets. He might even design an improved netting needle for you!

A DAY IN THE LIFE OF A REGENCY LADY

7 A.M.: Rise.

7–7:30 A.M.: Wash, tidy your hair, dress.

7:30–8 A.M.: Meet with your housekeeper, choose dinner menu.

8–9 A.M.: Look in on the nursery; make sure the children are awake, washed, dressed, fed, and usefully employed.

9–10 A.M.: Practice your instrument.

10–11 A.M.: Breakfast.

11 A.M.–3 P.M.: Pay morning calls or stay in and receive your own callers. Between calls, take care of darning and other family sewing. While guests are present, do only fancy needlework.

3–4 P.M.: Tend to your correspondence: Write letters and answer invitations.

4–5 P.M.: Play with the children or read an improving book.

5–6 P.M.: Retire to your dressing room to rest and dress for dinner.

6–8 P.M.: Dine.

8–11 P.M.: Spend time with your family or guests you have invited to dine or drink tea.

11–11:30 P.M.: Undress and prepare for bed.

11:30 P.M.: Retire.

- *Knotting.* Using silk or cotton thread wound onto an oval-shaped shuttle, tie a series of knots to create a decorative trim or fringe. Using the couching method, sew the trim carefully to fabric that will be used to upholster furniture or make curtains or other household items. When finished, the fabric will look as though it has been embroidered with French knots.

- *Tambour work.* Stretch fabric tightly over a hoop, then use a long, thin hook to draw fine thread through the fabric to make a chain stitch in a pretty design. This kind of embroidery looks lovely on a ball gown. Crochet, or "tambour in the air," is a descendant of this art.

HOW TO MAKE A FILIGREE BASKET

Many a refined Regency lady spends her downtime practicing the art of paper filigree. Also known as quilling, paper filigree is a decorative craft that involves rolling up thin strips of colored paper into spirals and arranging them in attractive designs.

WHAT YOU WILL NEED:
- Gold or silver paper cut into $1/8$ inch-wide strips (you can use another color if you prefer, but gold and silver are festive and pretty)
- A quill feather (not a pen; the end should be intact)
- Wooden or paper basket
- Paste (have the cook boil it up from flour and water)
- A small paintbrush

1. **Wrap the coil.** Take a strip of gold paper and wrap the short end tightly around the end of the quill *(Fig. G)*. Keep wrapping until the entire strip is coiled around the quill *(Fig. H)*.

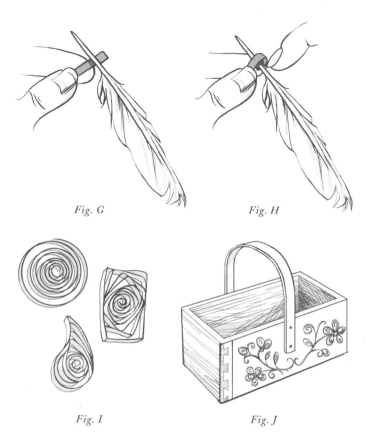

Fig. G

Fig. H

Fig. I

Fig. J

2. **Set the coil.** Hold the paper roll for a minute or so. If you want the coil to be tight, hold onto it as you slide it off the end of the quill. If you want the coil to expand, let go and it will expand and slip off the quill.

3. **Shape the coil.** You can change the shape of the coil by pinching one end to make a teardrop, or both ends to make

a diamond shape. Squares, triangles, and other shapes can be made using the same method.

4. **Make several different shapes** *(Fig. I)*. Try rolling each end of a strip of paper in different directions for a pretty, swirly shape. Use shorter strips of paper to make smaller coils.

5. **Lay out the design.** Arrange the coils on the tabletop or a piece of scrap paper and move them around until you find a design that you like. Experiment with different shapes and coil tension to find the prettiest effect.

6. **Paste the coils to the basket.** When you have decided on your design, brush a little paste onto one side of the coils and place them on the basket. You do not have to cover the whole basket; sometimes a minimalist look is just as pretty.

7. **Wait for the paste to dry thoroughly.** Leave it at least overnight. If possible, give the paste a week to cure thoroughly.

8. **Apply the finishing touches.** You may paint it if you like, but if you used pretty paper, painting is unnecessary.

9. **Give the basket** *(Fig. J)* **to a friend.**

HOW A GENTLEMAN SPENDS HIS LEISURE TIME

Fox hunting: Begins in late October and continues through March. Requires a sizable outlay of cash for horses and equipment, and wealthy neighbors to sponsor the hunt.

Shooting: Starts in late August, when grouse season opens, and continues through January. The dogs flush the birds with help from the beaters, who raise the coveys so the birds fly into the air where they can be sighted and shot.

Fishing: Season runs from early spring through late autumn. Includes fly-fishing for trout on a river or stream, or coarse fishing for pike and eel in a pond or lake.

Playing billiards: When outdoor sports are unseasonable, many gentlemen occupy themselves at the billiards table. Many houses have a small room set aside for this purpose, which is exclusively male territory.

Maintaining the family library: Books bound in cardboard are purchased and sent to a bookbinder to be bound in leather with gilt ends.

Attending clubs: In the city, many gentlemen belong to eating clubs such as White's, Brooks's, or Boodle's. In the country, gentlemen might have a local eating club or whist club that meets once or twice weekly.

Boxing and fencing: The well-known fencing instructor Henry Angelo and the retired boxing champion John "Gentleman" Jackson share premises at No. 13 Bond Street in London, where they instruct gentlemen in their respective arts.

LADY MIGHT EARN A LIVING
(IF NECESSARY)

JANE FAIRFAX: *"I am not at all afraid of being long unemployed. There are places in town, offices, where inquiry would soon produce something—Offices for the sale—not quite of human flesh—but of human intellect."*
MRS. ELTON: *"Oh! my dear, human flesh! You quite shock me; if you mean a fling at the slave-trade, I assure you Mr. Suckling was always rather a friend to the abolition."* —EMMA

It is a truth universally acknowledged that in this world there are haves and have-nots. Some are born to marry a man with ten thousand a year and have jewels and pin money second to none; some are destined to teach that woman's children and be patronized by her servants. In the sad event that you are forced to seek employment, here are a few acceptable ways for you to do so. All are ill-paid and unpleasant in their own way and should be avoided if at all possible.

🌀 **Governess.** You will have the charge of the daughters and sometimes the very young sons of the house, acting as their teacher, chaperone, psychologist, and older sister. If you are very fortunate, you will be treated as a member of the family, but in most cases you will be ignored by the adults of the household and treated with affectionate disrespect by the children. The servants will say that you "put on airs" and want nothing to do with you, so unless the daughters are a little older and good companions, this can be a lonely proposition.

Schoolteacher. Rather like being a governess. Your living arrangements might be less comfortable, but teaching at a school offers more autonomy than living in someone else's home.

Companion. Because it is unseemly for unmarried females to live alone, a single lady might hire another woman to live with her. Sometimes these females in search of a companion are very young ladies, not yet out in society; sometimes they are older ladies, who never married and whose parents have passed away. This position is not unlike being relegated to the status of "poor relation"—one is never allowed to forget that one is dependent and must put up with the whims and megrims of one's employer without comment. A companion to a very young lady will act as a sort of governess, who will be held responsible for her behavior.

Lady's maid. If one has a good sense of style, one might become a personal maid to a fine lady. You will help her choose her wardrobe to suit her figure and coloring, and sometimes make up the clothes for her, or at least update older pieces to suit changing fashions. You should be able to sew a fine seam, make over clothes, and style hair. You will be allowed to keep your mistress's discarded clothing, which you either can wear yourself or sell for extra money.

Authoress. A risky undertaking, because if your book does not sell well, you will be responsible for the cost of printing. Also, depending on the sort of book one writes, this is not the most respectable profession for a lady. You can publish anonymously, to keep your privacy, but the secret may get out eventually, especially if you have proud family members who want to tell the world. Despite the potential drawbacks, this profession will give one the most autonomy.

THE SMELL OF THE SHOP

The gentry of Jane Austen's novels were in a sort of half-world between the aristocracy and the bourgeois middle class. If one earned a fortune in trade, or better yet, if one's ancestors had, one's manners and lifestyle could gain one acceptance into good society, and personal connections counted for even more.

In *Emma*, Mr. Weston had made his fortune in trade, but the snobbish Emma Woodhouse was happy to invite him to her home, probably because he was married to her former governess. She was a little more particular about accepting an invitation to dine with the Coles, a local family who had made a fortune in trade but were still clawing their way up the social ladder. Someone like Mr. Gardiner in *Pride and Prejudice*, who lived "within sight of his warehouses," was right on the edge. When he first thought of marrying Elizabeth Bennet, Mr. Darcy considered the Gardiners beneath his notice, but when he met them and saw that they had well-bred manners, he was happy to welcome them into his family. (Elizabeth's scolding after he first proposed marriage might have had something to do with that, too.)

ACCEPTABLE MEN'S PROFESSIONS

⬤ **The church.** After attending one of the universities, a man was ordained as a deacon at age twenty-three, assisting an ordained priest, then fully ordained at twenty-four, allowing him to administer sacraments. He still had to secure a "living," or a position in a parish. As rector of a parish, he collected both great tithes (10 percent of the cereal crops grown in the parish) and small tithes (10 percent of the parish's produce and livestock). Vicars were entitled only to the small tithes. Rectors also received glebe land, farmland that he either worked himself or rented out.

⬤ **The military.** The military, especially the navy, was excellent for younger sons or those in need of discipline. Until they achieved high rank, however, they still needed some support from their families; their pay was unlikely to cover their expenses, and they needed assistance in purchasing commissions or obtaining inluence for higher-ranking positions.

⬤ **The law.** An aspiring attorney studied at one of the Inns of Court in London, apprenticing with members of the bar and eventually taking cases of his own as he worked toward becoming a barrister.

⬤ **Medicine.** Physicians received a degree from one of the universities and served an apprenticeship with an established medical man. Some of the more dedicated attended the medical school in Edinburgh, but it was generally thought an unnecessary step.

DRESS

*Dress was her passion. She had a most harmless
delight in being fine.* —NORTHANGER ABBEY

Purchasing clothing is not as easy as going into a shop and choosing something off the rack, and with two or three clothing changes called for daily, dressing properly is a subject that requires close attention.

● **Morning dress** *(Fig. A).* Simple styles and sturdier fabrics are best for morning wear, which is worn from the time one gets up until dinner. Plain or sprigged muslins in light colors or darker-colored calico or wool are best for your morning gowns. Because showing your bosom is inappropriate during the day, wear a chemisette, a half shirt rather like a dickey, under your gown, or tuck a fichu, a triangular piece of lace, netting, or gauze, around your neck and into your bodice *(Fig. A-1).* Either can later be switched out, giving an old dress a fresh new look. If you are married or do not wish to fuss with your hair, wear a cap, but be aware that it telegraphs that you are unavailable for marriage.

● **Evening dress** *(Fig. B).* For dinner and afterwards, change into something truly elegant and perhaps even a little daring. Evening is the time for your flimsiest muslins, prettiest trimmings, and whatever family jewelry you can wheedle out of your mother. Low-cut bodices are perfectly acceptable, and a pretty headdress or some beads or flowers woven into your hair will add just the right touch. Younger ladies should stick with muslin gowns, while married or older

ladies can wear gowns made of light silk. And remember—
a woman can never look too fine when she is all in white.

◉ **Undergarments** *(Fig. C)*. Wearing the correct undergarments
  is important to give your gowns the proper fit and shape.
  • *First layer—the shift (Fig. C-1)*. Next to your skin, wear a
    shift, a basic sack dress with a drawstring neckline and
    that falls to just above the knee. In addition to providing
    warmth and modesty, shifts keep clothing cleaner by keep-
    ing finer fabrics off the skin.
  • *Second layer—stays (Fig. C-2)*. On top of the shift, wear

WOMEN'S UNDERWEAR

Ladies generally did not wear drawers in Jane
Austen's day. After all, what would a well-bred
lady be doing that required more coverage for
her private parts than a close-fitting floor-
length gown provided? Drawers did not come
into wide use until crinolines became fashionable in the 1850s, when a gust of wind easily
could blow a lady's skirt up over her head.
Some of the very fast and fashionable set did
wear various kinds of drawers in the Regency,
but they were considered a bit risqué.

That means we may indeed assume, with a
high degree of probability, that Jane Austen
went commando.

your stays, or corset, to give support to the bust and smooth the torso. Your maid will tie your laces in the back. They should be firmly tied but not so tight that you cannot breathe. Insert the busk, a long, thin strip of bone, wood, or ivory, in the opening that runs along the breastbone to improve your posture.

- *Third layer—petticoat.* A "waist petticoat" (like a long half-slip), made of muslin or wool, might be worn under a sturdier gown for warmth or modesty *(Fig C-3)*. A petticoat can look like a gown by itself, and is worn as part of an outfit—for instance, a sleeveless gown in a complementary color worn under a transparently gauzy overdress or an open-front robe can be referred to as a petticoat. Such petticoats can be made of muslin or even silk, just like a regular gown.

🌊 **Outerwear** *(Fig. D).* Outerwear will not only keep you warm, but it is also as much of a style statement as your gowns.
- *Pelisse.* A long coat that can completely cover a gown, be cut away in front, or only reach to the knees.
- *Spencer (Fig. D-1).* A coat covering the sleeves and bodice of a high-waisted gown.
- *Cloak.* Hooded cloaks are usually worn over a skimpy ball gown for warmth, but woolen cloaks are also worn for daytime.

🌊 **Accessories.** Elegant accessories provide the perfect finishing touch to any outfit.
- *Gloves.* Wear gloves outside at all times for warmth and protection, even in summer; you do not want your hands tanned or freckled as though you work in the fields. Elbow-length white kid gloves should be worn for formal parties. When supper is served, unbutton them at the wrist, slip out your hands, and tuck the gloves back into

Fig. A   *Fig. B*

Fig. C   Fig. D

your wrist so that you do not drag them through the negus. Always wear gloves for dancing, as will your partner; after all, one would not wish to dance with some sweaty-pawed creature.

- *Shawl.* The cold winter weather makes a shawl a necessary accoutrement at all times when you are not sitting directly in front of a fire. Shawls made of cashmere wool from India, woven in intricate and colorful designs, are practical as well as beautiful. Lighter shawls of embroidered muslin or gauze can be welcome with ball gowns on chilly summer nights as well.

- *Hats and bonnets.* Wear a hat or bonnet when you go outside in daytime. Leave your bonnet on when paying a short call, but take it off if you mean to stay for a few hours. Do not wear a bonnet or hat to an evening party or ball, though a turban or fancy headdress is fine.

- *Caps.* Married ladies and spinsters who wish to indicate that they are not available for marriage wear caps made of muslin or lace with morning attire and sometimes for informal evening dress to keep their hair tidy.

- *Stockings.* Stockings can be very light silk for balls or knitted from wool for warmth in winter. They come to a little above the knee and are held up with garters, which might be knitted or just ribbons tied above the knee *(Fig C-4)*.

- *Footwear.* Half-boots for riding or walking; dainty slippers, like ballet slippers, for evening, sometimes with decorative roses on the toes. Some ladies wear pattens, wooden slats with metal rings on the bottom, to keep their footwear out of muddy roads.

◉ **Active wear.** Ladies have special clothing for riding and more strenuous outdoor activities.

- *Riding habit.* A habit is worn for horseback riding, of course, but it can also be worn for traveling or even just around the house for morning wear. Habits are made of sturdy fabrics, fitted like a long coat, and are sometimes a little longer or fuller on one side to accommodate riding sidesaddle. Wear a chemisette with a frilled collar underneath to protect your neck from the sun, and if you are riding, wear a riding hat with a veil to keep insects and dirt out of your eyes. If you are just wearing your habit for traveling or walking, you can wear it with a regular bonnet.

- *Walking dresses:* A walking dress is like a riding habit, but with fancier trim and worn with a regular bonnet.

Mourning clothes. Mourning clothes are made of bombazine, a silk and wool mix, or crepe, a crinkly black silk, both of which have a dull finish. Crepe also is used to trim headwear. According to custom, widows should wear mourning dress for twelve months, children for six months, and siblings for three months. For the first half of that time period, referred to as the first mourning, wear full mourning dress, or all black; for the second half, or second mourning, wear one black article of clothing along with white, gray, or lilac. Mourning jewelry such as a ring or brooch with a lock of the deceased's hair is also worn. For more distant relations, wear black gloves or ribbons or a crepe band on your hat for a few weeks or months, depending on the closeness of the connection, as a sign of respect.

Wedding clothes. A woman's father traditionally gives her money to purchase enough clothing to last her a year so she will not put her new husband to immediate expense for her clothing. For the wedding itself, the bride will purchase a new gown that she will wear afterwards for other suitable occasions. The white wedding gown is not compulsory, but since white is such a popular color for gowns anyway, many wedding dresses are white or cream-colored. Wear a pretty bonnet or a hat with a veil attached to the back.

MEN'S ATTIRE

Like women's clothing, menswear underwent a change at the close of the eighteenth century, moving away from the formal silks and laces of the French court. Men's fashions are reminiscent of the clothing British men wear for country sports.

🕉 **Morning dress.** In the daytime, a gentleman will wear a cutaway coat in a plain dark fabric, a style just made for riding on horseback, as well as a waistcoat, breeches or pantaloons, boots, and a snowy linen shirt and cravat.

🕉 **Evening dress** *(Fig. E).* For formal evening parties, coats are basic black, worn with a waistcoat *(Fig. E-1)*, knee breeches *(Fig. E-2)*, white stockings, and black shoes with gold or silver buckles. Linen shirts must be spotlessly clean and crisply ironed.

🕉 **Undergarments.** Traditionally, a gentleman did not wear drawers—instead, he simply crossed the trailing ends of his shirt underneath his crotch inside his breeches or pantaloons. However, as cleanliness becomes more the fashion, more men have taken to wearing knee-length drawers of a knit material to keep breeches or pantaloons from directly touching the skin. These drawers are tied with corset-like strings at the back waist for a close fit and buttoned at the waist, with an opening in the front for convenience.

Fig. E

◉ **Outerwear.** For cold weather, every gentleman has a great coat; younger men wear them with as many as sixteen capes around the shoulders to keep out cold, snow, and rain while driving an open vehicle.

◉ **Accessories.**
- *Hats.* High-crowned hats are worn outdoors; for evening, a gentleman tucks a chapeau-bras or bicorne hat beneath his arm.
- *Jewelry.* A tasteful watch and fob and perhaps a jeweled pin in the cravat are generally worn both for evening and non-active morning wear, though more foppish gentlemen might accessorize with seals dangling from their watch fob and snuffboxes made of precious metals or painted porcelain.
- *Cravat (Fig. E-3).* Made of spotlessly clean starched muslin, usually white, and tied in any number of fashionable methods.
- *Walking stick.* In the city, every gentleman has a sleek, elegant walking stick. In the country, a sturdy branch will do to assist one in walking up muddy hills. When paying a morning call, it is impolite to leave one's hat or walking stick anywhere in the house, lest one be suspected of planning to overstay one's welcome.

◉ **Hairstyles.** The taxation of hair powder spurred an au naturel trend in men's hairstyles; like the ladies, men's hairstyles tend to imitate classical statuary, with some gentlemen even sporting an exaggerated windblown look.

LADIES' HAIRSTYLES, MAKEUP, & BEAUTY TREATMENTS

Powdering the hair was already passing from fashion when a tax on hair powder in 1795 rang the death knell; thereafter, only patriotic old Tories still used the stuff. Early in the period, young women often wore their hair in long curls for the proper romantic look, with ribbons or beads twined through their hair for the evening. Around the start of the nineteenth century, ladies began wearing their hair up off their nape, with a few curly locks loose around their face. Hair was also occasionally worn short, cropped close to the head, and worn either sleek or curly.

For makeup, the natural look was the order of the day—the heavily powdered and rouged look of the eighteenth century was abandoned. However, that did not mean that ladies used no cosmetics at all. Jane Austen's close friend and housemate, Martha Lloyd, compiled a book of recipes that contained several beauty preparations, including milk of roses, used as a skin lotion; hand soap and softening pomatum; cold cream made of wax, spermaceti (whale oil), oil of sweet almonds, and rosewater; coral tooth powder; and lavender water, which was used both as a perfume and to revive those who had fainted.

In *Persuasion*, Sir Walter Elliot, who is very attentive to everyone's looks, encourages Mrs. Clay to use Gowland's Lotion and opines that Lady Russell should use rouge during daylight hours. Gowland's Lotion was a commercial preparation that contained mercuric chloride, which acted as a chemical peel. No wonder he found ladies' skin to be "fresher" after they used it! One rather wonders whether the extremely vain Sir Walter used a touch of Gowland's himself.

BUY CLOTHING

I shall want two coloured gowns for the summer, for my pink one will not do more than clear me from Steventon. I shall not trouble you, however, to get more than one of them, and that is to be a plain brown cambric muslin, for morning wear; the other, which is to be a very pretty yellow and white cloud, I mean to buy in Bath. —LETTER FROM JANE AUSTEN TO CASSANDRA AUSTEN, JANUARY 25, 1801

It pays to be thoroughly prepared when shopping for clothes. Fashions change quickly, and one will always want to be up on the latest look. But one can only buy ready-made gowns secondhand, and who wants to wear some other person's castoffs? Therefore, here is some guidance for how you might spend your pin money wisely.

1. **Take inventory.** Go through your existing wardrobe and determine what you need for the coming season.

2. **Research.** Study *Ackermann's Repository*, *The Gallery of Fashion*, or other stylish publications to see what is being worn. Consult with friends and relatives who live in London or have spent time there recently. They will be able to tell you the latest cuts of sleeves and bodices and how gowns and bonnets are being trimmed.

3. **Acquire patterns.** If a friend or acquaintance has a gown that you particularly admire, ask if you can make a pattern from it. Cut out fabric in the shapes of the gown's pieces, baste the fabric pieces together so they can be taken apart

easily, and reserve it as your "pattern gown." Reciprocate this favor not just for gowns, but for baby clothes, caps, and other items.

4. **Purchase fabric.** Go to the local linen draper and choose fabric. You'll need seven to ten yards of fabric to make a gown. Leftover fabric can be used to make over old gowns or for handkerchiefs, caps, and other accessories; muslin can never be said to be wasted. Choose trimming to dress up the gown if desired. You may ask a friend or relative who is living in a larger town or city to pick up something particular for you, but only if you trust her taste.

5. **Consult the professionals.** Visit your mantua-maker (dress-maker) and give her your pattern gown or show her the fashion plates you like so she can sketch out a style. Leave the fabric and trimming with her. Your new gown should be ready within a week—less if she has seamstresses on staff.

6. **Renew and recycle.** To further extend your wardrobe, go over what you already have that is still in good shape. Make it over, add a flounce, dye it, or add new trimming to freshen it up and bring it into the latest style.

7. **Accessorize.** New outerwear will give life to a wardrobe—purchase a new pelisse or reline one that you already have.

INFLUENCES ON EARLY NINETEENTH-CENTURY CLOTHING

Neoclassicism: Architecture and interior design reflected society's interest in ancient Greece and Rome, and ladies' fashion followed; waistlines rose, gowns became more diaphanous and clinging, and hair was piled high on the crown with ringlets around the face in imitation of classical statuary. The Greek key motif was often used on trimmings.

The French Revolution: Once King Louis and Marie Antoinette lost their heads, society threw off their elaborate brocades and high wigs for dress that imitated the simpler clothing of the revolutionaries. English patriotism also directed a change away from the clothing worn by the French enemy to simpler homegrown styles, such as the outfits men wore for hunting, or informal women's morning gowns.

George "Beau" Brummell: A crony of the Prince Regent, Brummell was one of the main arbiters of style until debt and a falling-out with the Regent forced him to retire to France in 1816. "The Beau" preferred simple styles perfectly cut and made up in quality fabrics, and society copied his example. He hated the filthiness of the elaborate eighteenth-century costumes and hairstyles. He bathed daily and kept his clothing scrupulously clean, and fortunately for everyone, society copied that practice as well. He was also meticulous in his personal presentation—he often discarded a dozen clean, ironed cravats each day as he tied and retied the knot until he considered the knot to be perfect.

Britain in the world: As merchants explored and the army and navy fought in the far corners of the earth, they brought back fabrics and styles that had never been seen before. Exotic items such as cashmere shawls became commonplace, and victories in battle inspired fashion; even Jane Austen succumbed, borrowing a "Mamalouc cap," a sort of turban, from a friend to wear to a ball after the Royal Navy defeated Napoleon at the Battle of the Nile. Military-style trim on ladies' outerwear was common around the time of the Battle of Waterloo in 1815.

SECTION III:

Making Love

CHOOSE A PROSPECTIVE HUSBAND

Tell Mary that I make over Mr. Heartley & all his Estate to her for her sole use and Benefit in future, & not only him, but all my other Admirers into the bargain wherever she can find them, even the kiss which C. Powlett wanted to give me, as I mean to confine myself in future to Mr. Tom Lefroy, for whom I do not care sixpence. —LETTER FROM JANE AUSTEN TO CASSANDRA AUSTEN, JANUARY 14, 1796

As a Regency lady, choosing a husband is the most important decision you will make in your life. Once you're married, you're stuck with him. Divorce is possible but extremely difficult and expensive, especially for women; in most marriages, men control the fortune. And while a rich man with a fancy estate is all very well—and indeed one should not marry a poor man—do some soul-searching before you accept, and go into the match with your eyes wide open. Ask yourself the following questions—and answer them honestly!

❁ **Does he have a good income?** While one should not mind being asked to economize a little, one would not wish to be put to constant pains to contrive the elegancies of life.

❁ **Does he have good principles?** Bad boys are all very well for girlhood crushes, but do not marry one with the idea that you might "change" him. He will spend all your father's money and leave you at home with the children. Find a good man and treasure him.

MARRYING FOR MONEY VS. MARRYING FOR LOVE

Not long before Jane Austen's time, the upper classes did not choose a mate on the basis of attraction or affection. One great fortune looked for another, and if affection came into play as well, it was merely a lucky coincidence. However, the nineteenth century brought new ideas, and a heroine could at last declare, as did Emma Watson in Jane Austen's unfinished work *The Watsons*, that she "would rather be Teacher at a school (and I can think of nothing worse) than marry a Man I did not like."

Elizabeth Bennet's offer from Mr. Collins in *Pride and Prejudice* would have been a very good one in the eyes of her contemporaries, and better than she could expect given her lack of inheritance. And her initial rejection of Mr. Darcy, a very rich man, was even more outrageous in view of the common wisdom of the day. However, the reader understands that Jane Austen approves of Elizabeth's refusals because she should not marry a man she does not respect. If she had done so, she would be repeating her father's mistake, and certain to end up unhappy.

Jane herself was faced with a similar choice when Harris Bigg-Wither, the heir to a large estate, made her an offer of marriage. If she had accepted, she was guaranteed lifetime security for herself and her family. Jane actually did accept Harris's proposal, then changed her mind overnight, allowing us to be very sure of Jane Austen's opinion of marriages made only for financial motives.

🌸 **Is he handsome?** He should be, if at all possible—or at least very near it.

🌸 **Is he a sensible man?** One would not wish for a silly or stupid husband. However, if one wishes only for an establishment of one's own, at least be sure he is not stubborn as well. If he is easily controlled, you can contrive to almost entirely avoid being in his company.

🌸 **Does he have a sense of humor?** If not, you will need to teach him to be laughed at. If your manners are lively and easy, this will complement his gravity well. In fact, that is probably what made you attractive to him.

🌸 **Does he love you?** You do not want to marry a man who only is marrying you for fortune or position, because he feels an obligation towards you, or because of a passing infatuation. When these quick passions wear off, your life together may become intolerable. If you cannot love your husband, at least you should be able to respect your partner in life.

🌸 **Do you love him?** The most important question of all. Your choice in a husband may provide you with more fine clothes and fine carriages than your sisters and friends, but will they make you happy? If he is a good man, and has made you love him, then your chance for a happy marriage is very good indeed.

INDICATE INTEREST IN A GENTLEMAN WITHOUT SEEMING FORWARD

MISS BINGLEY: *"I am afraid you do not like your pen. Let me mend it for you. I mend pens remarkably well."*
MR. DARCY: *"Thank you—but I always mend my own."*
—*PRIDE AND PREJUDICE*

In a time when communication between unmarried persons of the opposite sex is so proscribed by social mores, it is difficult to let a man know that you find him attractive. In nine cases out of ten, a woman had better show *more* affection than she feels, because a man's own natural diffidence might lead him to think that she is not interested in him otherwise. But how to do so and maintain your reputation? Read on for some techniques that will get the point across—unless he is a blockhead, of course. But you wouldn't want to marry a blockhead, anyway.

- **Flatter his vanity.** Listen to everything he says with great interest, admire everything he does, and agree with him on all subjects. If he disagrees with something you have said, turn your own

words around so you sound as though you actually agree
with him.

⚜ **Talk about him to his relatives.** They might take the hint
and pass it on to him. You know how siblings like to tease!

⚜ **Offer to perform little services for him.** Mending his pen
might be one step from mending his stockings.

⚜ **Ask him if he would like to go "stargazing."** Everyone
knows what that means. If not, he must be rather clueless,
and perhaps you should rethink your affection.

⚜ **Keep your cool.** If he shows interest in another young lady,
pretend that you do not care. Tease him about his
"conquest" and ask when you might wish him joy.

⚜ **Mirror his actions.** If he is reading a book, take up the
second volume. If he is playing cards, help make up his
table. If he is going for a walk, declare that it is time for
your daily stroll in the shrubbery.

⚜ **Find him irresistible.** You will become so yourself.

MARRY OFF YOUR DAUGHTER

Mrs. Norris was most zealous in promoting the match,
by every suggestion and contrivance likely to enhance
its desirableness to either party. —MANSFIELD PARK

As a mother, it is the business of your life to see your daughters married, and if you can offer assistance to your nieces in that capacity, all the better. Even though you may not wish to be going out in public quite as much as when you were younger, nothing should stand in your way when it comes to launching your girls.

1. **Identify a likely suitor.** Pay attention to your daughter's dance partners for likely prospects at social gatherings. Determine which ones she seems to like best, and weed out the fortune hunters, half-pay officers, and other undesirable candidates.

2. **Cultivate his mother.** She is as concerned in this matter as you are—and it is always better to get along well with your in-laws.

3. **Invite the prospect to your social gatherings.** Provide opportunities for your daughter to become better acquainted with her potential husband by inviting him to dinner and evening parties. Feed him well and his heart will no doubt follow. Make sure that he knows that your daughter will be able to provide the same kind of excellent dinners for him and his guests.

4. **Chase off the competition.** If he is a desirable partner, there will be other mothers sniffing around, hoping to snag him for their daughter or niece. Run them off! You were there first!

5. **Talk up your daughter at every opportunity.** Let the gentleman and his friends know how difficult it will be for you to part with your angel, but assure them that you will do it for her own good in the face of such an excellent match.

6. **Give your daughter a taste of what she can look forward to.** Arrange a trip to her suitor's house and make sure there is someone to show you around. Encourage your daughter to imagine herself as mistress of the house.

7. **Contrive to leave the couple alone together.** Invite him to your home, then summon your other daughters to your dressing room one by one so your plan is not too obvious.

Do not let them resist the summons; if you have raised them to be dutiful daughters, they will do as they are bid. Time alone will provide him with the opportunity to propose.

8. **Remind your daughter of the advantages of the match.** Tell her how rich and how great she will be. Point out the carriages and pin money that will be at her disposal. What young lady can resist such an argument?

9. **Remind her of her duty.** If she is a do-gooder type, remind her that she has a duty to her family to marry well and take care of her widowed mother and orphaned sisters once your husband is deceased.

10. **Prevent your husband from talking her out of it.** You know what's best for your own daughter, after all. If a man has twelve thousand a year, it doesn't matter if he is stupid.

11. **Threaten her if necessary.** If the silly girl refuses to marry a perfectly acceptable young man because he is stupid or for some other trifling reason, explain to her that you will never speak to her again if she does not marry him.

12. **Cry at her wedding.** After all your hard work to promote the match, you deserve the release!

IS MRS. BENNET THE HERO OF PRIDE AND PREJUDICE?

Some Austen scholars have said that Mrs. Bennet is the real hero of *Pride and Prejudice*, because she alone seems to understand her daughters' desperate situation. Had Mr. Bennet died before the girls were married, they would have little fortune and no home except at the questionable mercy of Mr. Collins. The scholars argue that Mr. Bennet's indolent ways and failure to plan for his daughters placed them in a difficult position, and Mrs. Bennet had every right to be angry with Elizabeth for refusing Mr. Collins.

However, contrasting the reactions of Elizabeth's parents at the news of her engagement to Mr. Darcy can be illuminating. Mr. Bennet does not know that Lizzy has fallen in love with Mr. Darcy and tries to dissuade her, not wanting his favorite daughter to repeat his mistake of marrying unwisely. But once Elizabeth expresses her feelings toward Darcy, he gives his blessing. Despite his failings, Mr. Bennet has his child's happiness as his first consideration.

Mrs. Bennet, who is equally unaware of Elizabeth's change of heart, is rude to Darcy, but when Elizabeth shares the news of her engagement she is delighted. "Oh! my sweetest Lizzy! how rich and how great you will be!" she cries. "What pin-money, what jewels, what carriages you will have!" She is concerned only with money, not with wise marriage, and this reaction echoes her happiness at Lydia's unwise marriage to Mr. Wickham. Mrs. Bennet wants her daughters to marry because it increases her own consequence, not because she truly cares about the girls' welfare.

How to

DECLINE AN UNWANTED PROPOSAL OF MARRIAGE

She believed he had been drinking too much of Mr. Weston's good wine, and felt sure that he would want to be talking nonsense. —EMMA

You have had some hints that a particular gentleman has developed an interest in you; the problem is that you cannot stand him because he is stupid, disagreeable, abominably proud, or just plain creepy. While it is true that a man has the power of choice, a woman has the power of refusal. Start off gently; if he does not take the hint, work your way up to letting him have it in a raking broadside.

🌹 **Head him off at the pass.** Let his sister or another relative know that you are not interested. With luck, they will get the message across before it becomes an issue.

🌹 **Be an ice queen.** If he does not make a plain proposal, behave as though you are insulted by his creepy hints.

🌹 **Play the ingénue.** Pretend that you do not understand him. If he comes back later and claims that you accepted him, you can say that you do not know what he is talking about.

🌹 **Be firm.** No means no! If he presses you, keep telling him no until he finally understands, or at least leaves you alone.

🌹 **Distract him.** Introduce him to a girlfriend who is not as picky as you are.

WORST (AND FUNNIEST) PROPOSALS IN JANE AUSTEN'S NOVELS

John Thorpe to Catherine Morland in *Northanger Abbey*: Blustering braggart John Thorpe tries to let Catherine Morland know that he wants to marry her, but does such a hilariously poor job of it that Catherine has no idea that he has made a declaration. Of course, when a girl has Henry Tilney on the brain, who can blame her?

Mr. Collins to Elizabeth Bennet in *Pride and Prejudice*: Elizabeth Bennet's cousin Mr. Collins, who will inherit her father's estate, thinks it proper to marry one of the daughters of the house, and chooses Elizabeth rather arbitrarily, despite their complete lack of compatibility. Even Elizabeth is hard put not to laugh when he talks about being run away with his feelings in his solemn, pompous manner. Elizabeth is relatively gracious in her refusal, but Mr. Collins's refusal to accept her refusal, insisting that she is being coy, is pure comedy.

Mr. Darcy to Elizabeth Bennet in *Pride and Prejudice*: There's nothing like insulting your potential bride's family as you ask for a girl's hand to make her fall in a swoon at your feet. But Darcy redeemed himself by taking Elizabeth's constructive criticism to heart and did much better with his second proposal, sealing the deal with "dearest, loveliest Elizabeth." What woman could resist?

Mr. Elton to Emma Woodhouse in *Emma*: Emma Woodhouse's matchmaking scheme goes comically awry when the man she had intended for her protégée Harriet Smith thinks he is being encouraged to propose to Emma herself. Mr. Elton does not take rejection well, and his continuing rude behavior as the novel progresses convinces readers that Mr. Elton gets the bride he deserves in the obnoxious Augusta Hawkins.

Mr. Elliot to Anne Elliot in *Persuasion*: During the concert scene at the Assembly Rooms, Anne's cousin, the handsome Mr. Elliot, drops broad hints that he wants to marry her. Anne is in love with Captain Wentworth and distrusts the secretive Mr. Elliot, so she finds these comments distressing—even more so when Captain Wentworth leaves the concert in a fit of jealousy. Not only are Mr. Elliot's hints creepy, but since his first wife had been dead for only a few months, they are vulgar as well.

Henry Crawford to Fanny Price in *Mansfield Park*: Mr. Crawford is a master manipulator who sees every woman's weakness and exploits it. In Fanny Price's case, he uses her love for her brother and her dependent situation to try to persuade her into marriage. Considering the differences in their ideas of morality and propriety, Fanny might have ended up very unhappy indeed had she accepted him.

🌀 **Insult him.** You never know, he might take your words to heart and turn himself into quite a good catch!

🌀 **Swoon.** Always effective, but be sure to use this tactic only as a last resort.

How to

CARRY ON A
SECRET ENGAGEMENT

MARIANNE DASHWOOD: *"But why were you not there,*
Edward?—Why did you not come?"
EDWARD FERRARS: *"I was engaged elsewhere."*
MARIANNE: *"Engaged! But what was that, when such*
friends were to be met?"
LUCY STEELE: *"Perhaps, Miss Marianne,"* cried Lucy, eager
to take some revenge on her, *"you think young men never stand*
upon engagements, if they have no mind to keep them, little
as well as great." —SENSE AND SENSIBILITY

He did it—he popped the question. You are all happiness until
a cloud dulls the sunshine of your tender young love. His family does not approve. But he's sure he can talk them into it if
you just give him some time. He will contrive a way to introduce you into the family, and once they know you, they are
sure to love you as he does!

Fortunately for you, the law is on your side, as well as society. If he breaks it off, not only will his honor be questionable, but your father can bring suit for breach of promise. All
is well so long as you have no reason to doubt his affection,
but if he becomes distracted, you will need to remind him of
his commitments.

◉ **Correspond regularly.** Keep yourself fresh in his mind.
Because you are engaged, there is nothing wrong with
exchanging letters, and they will serve as proof of your
engagement. So that your engagement is not discovered
before the time is right, you might be put to some pains to

pick up the mail yourself at the post office. Just tell everyone that you need the daily walk.

◉ **Provide him with a token of your affection.** A lock of your hair set into a ring is an excellent and ever-present reminder of your love for him. If he is tempted to speak with other young ladies, they will no doubt be curious about it, which will serve as a reminder of to whom his loyalty belongs.

◉ **Chase off poachers.** Do not be afraid to let other young ladies in on the secret if they show an interest in your young man. Appeal to their honor to keep the news in the strictest of confidence.

◉ **Contrive to be near him.** No doubt there will be some time when you can be alone together.

◉ **Distract the nosy parkers.** If someone appears to be suspicious of your relationship, throw her off the scent by suggesting that your beloved actually is in love with someone else entirely. Everyone loves gossip, and if you are sufficiently convincing, she will never suspect that you have thrown your dearest one under the stagecoach.

◉ **Threaten to break off the engagement.** If he gives you a bad time, let him know that you do not need him. You don't need a man; you can support yourself. Get yourself a position as a governess or companion; that will fix his little red wagon! But remember, angry people are not always wise. You might later regret a hasty, ill-considered action.

GET HIM BACK AFTER YOU HAVE QUARRELED

*He had not forgiven Anne Elliot. She had used him ill,
deserted and disappointed him; and worse, she had shewn a
feebleness of character in doing so, which his own decided,
confident temper could not endure. She had given him up to
oblige others. It had been the effect of over-persuasion. It
had been weakness and timidity. He had been most warmly
attached to her, and had never seen a woman since whom he
thought her equal; but, except from some natural sensation
of curiosity, he had no desire of meeting her again. Her
power with him was gone for ever. —PERSUASION*

At some point in every romance, there will be a little disagreement. Sometimes those little disagreements become large
ones, and you part in anger. Feelings of despair will naturally
follow, but after the first flush of emotion passes, more practical
concerns come to the fore. Have you lost him forever? Most
likely not, but with some compromise and changes on both
sides, your relationship can be more intense than ever after a
disagreement, even eight and a half years later. Here are some
techniques and tips to help you get past the Big Quarrel.

❂ **Forgive him.** If he has done something to anger you, give
   him the opportunity to show you that he has changed.

❂ **Communicate.** If he is laboring under a misapprehension,
   explain exactly what happened. Once he understands the
   situation, no doubt he will come around.

🌸 **Be patient.** Give him a chance to get over his anger. When he sees you in the company of other women, he will understand your true superiority.

🌸 **Accept constructive criticism.** Try to do better, and let him know that you are trying. You might come out of it a better person, and he will be pleased and proud that you have made an effort.

🌸 **Approach him through an intermediary.** If he will not listen to you, his sister or a friend might be willing to help.

🌸 **Trust him.** If he is the man you think he is, his good principles will see him through and bring him back to you.

🌸 **Fall into a decline.** Make yourself ill with unrequited love. He will hear of it and ride his horse into a lather to fling himself at your feet and beg your forgiveness. Just don't be so stupid as to actually die, especially if he has married someone else in the meantime.

🌸 **Wear nothing but his favorite color.** It may not become you, but no sacrifice is too great for the one you love.

BE A BRIDE

The wedding was very much like other weddings, where the parties have no taste for finery or parade; and Mrs. Elton, from the particulars detailed by her husband, thought it all extremely shabby, and very inferior to her own.— "Very little white satin, very few lace veils; a most pitiful business! Selina would stare when she heard of it."—But, in spite of these deficiencies, the wishes, the hopes, the confidence, the predictions of the small band of true friends who witnessed the ceremony, were fully answered in the perfect happiness of the union. —Emma

Everyone loves a story with a happy ending, and what ending can be happier than a wedding? While Regency weddings are small, simple affairs, a bride still has much to do in preparation for the day on which she will become the happiest of creatures.

THE ENGAGEMENT

1. **Ask permission.** Your fiancé must apply to your papa for permission to marry you if you are younger than twenty-one. If your beloved is younger than twenty-one, he must obtain permission from his own parents. Even if you are of age and consent is technically unnecessary, respectful children obtain their parents' blessing upon the union.

2. **Set the date.** To determine the best time for the wedding, consider your fiancé's obligations, your financial situation, the time it will take to prepare your wedding clothes, any transportation issues, and family concerns such as the care of elderly relatives. To obtain a proper, legally recognized marriage, you must wait a minimum of four weeks for the publication

of the banns (see Step 3) unless you have purchased a special license to marry without them. Long engagements are not common, and if there is nothing to wait for, fix an early date. You may be married on any day of the week, even Sunday immediately after the morning church service.

3. **Make it official.** Arrange to have the banns "published" in your parish—during the Sunday service for three weeks before the wedding is to take place, the presiding clergyman will ask the congregation if they know of any impediments to your marriage. If you are really in a hurry, you could purchase a special license from Doctor's Commons in London, the location of the ecclesiastical courts, which permits you to marry without declaring the banns (both parties must still be eligible to marry, though; no rushing into it if you're underage, you'll still need permission to proceed). Obtaining such a license can take a week or two, so unless there is some pressing reason, such as marrying outside your parish, it is unnecessary.

4. **Give your fiancé a small engagement gift.** A miniature portrait of you that he can wear next to his heart is an ideal token, as is a lock of your hair placed in a ring for him to wear. He will reciprocate the gesture, but do not expect to receive an expensive engagement ring. Such rings are not unknown, but they are not a common tradition.

5. **Purchase your wedding clothes.** Your father or guardian will give you money to purchase new clothes. If you live in the country, this is an excellent excuse for a prewedding trip to London or Bath, where you will have access to the best linen-drapers, milliners, and mantua-makers.

6. **Keep an eye on the negotiations.** With the assistance of their solicitors, your father and your future husband will

negotiate the marriage settlement. This settlement covers the financial aspects of your marriage, including the provisions for your children's inheritances, your support as a widow, and even your yearly allowance. It is wise to keep an eye on the proceedings, though ultimately you will have little control over the outcome.

7. **Choose your attendants.** You must have two official witnesses to your wedding to sign the parish register and in turn create the official record of your marriage. Traditionally, such witnesses are not yet married, so a younger eligible sister or two is a good choice. Give the attendants plenty of notice so they can acquire a new gown for the occasion, though they need not dress alike.

8. **Take leave of the neighborhood.** If your fiancé's estate is not in the same general area as your parents', call upon old neighbors during the week before the wedding to formally say farewell. Make plans for visits and correspondence with those to whom you are particularly close.

THE WEDDING DAY

1. **Make up your bouquet.** Pick wildflowers or something pretty from the garden, if it is summer; if not, hothouse flowers are acceptable. Wrap the stems in a pretty ribbon. Make up a little basket of flowers for your bridesmaid, too.

2. **Get to church bright and early.** By law, the ceremony must take place in your parish church before noon, unless you have purchased a special license (see Step 3, opposite). Your parents and attendant will drive to the church with you in the family carriage.

3. **Join your fiancé at the altar.** Your attendant will walk down

the aisle first. Then, either or both of your parents may escort you up the aisle, where your fiancé will be waiting with his attendant and the officiant. You will not have very many guests; probably just your immediate family and closest friends in the neighborhood.

4. **Conduct yourself with refinement and maturity.** As part of the ceremony, your new husband will say, "With my body I thee worship." Stifle the urge to giggle; it is most unladylike!

5. **Accept your fiancé's wedding ring.** The ring is an integral part of the Anglican sacrament of marriage; the ceremony cannot be performed without one. A plain gold band is the usual style. The groom's attendant will carry the ring and produce it when requested by the officiant. Men do not wear wedding rings.

6. **Do not kiss the groom!** Kissing in public, especially in a house of worship, would cause a scandal that never would be forgotten in the neighborhood. (However, what you do in a closed carriage on the way from the church to the wedding breakfast is your own affair—just don't let the servants see.)

7. **Sign the register.** This is the official public record of your marriage. Sign your maiden name for the last time. Your new husband and two witnesses will sign as well.

8. **Attend the wedding breakfast.** After the ceremony, join your family and friends at your parents' house for a celebratory meal of the usual breakfast foods: toast, rolls, eggs, cold meat, coffee, tea, and chocolate.

9. **Eat your wedding cake.** After breakfast, you and your guests

will share a fruitcake, often topped with marzipan icing and laced with brandy as a preservative. Send a slice of cake home with guests for those who were unable to attend the ceremony or breakfast. Each unmarried girl should take a slice and put it under her pillow so she will dream of the man she will marry.

10. **Include the whole household in your celebration.** Make sure that the servants have a bowl of (alcoholic) punch to make merry, and perhaps an especially nice supper and some wedding cake as well.

A REGENCY HONEYMOON

The honeymoon, or wedding tour, could last anywhere from a fortnight to several months. Because the European continent was embroiled in the Napoleonic wars at the time, newlyweds generally limited travel to Scotland, Ireland, Wales, the Lake Country, the Peak District, and the seaside. It was also common to visit the estates of various relatives so the new family member could be properly introduced and feted. Couples were often accompanied on their journey by a single sister or friend to keep the bride company on shopping trips and other purely feminine pursuits.

ELOPE TO SCOTLAND

I am going to Gretna Green, and if you cannot guess with who, I shall think you a simpleton, for there is but one man in the world I love, and he is an angel. I should never be happy without him, so think it no harm to be off. You need not send them word at Longbourn of my going, if you do not like it, for it will make the surprise the greater when I write to them and sign my name Lydia Wickham. What a good joke it will be! I can hardly write for laughing. —LETTER FROM LYDIA BENNET (NOT YET WICKHAM) IN *PRIDE AND PREJUDICE*

He is in a hurry to marry, and you not any less so, and no doubt your mother will approve—after all, she has been pestering you to get married since you came out, and she will help bring your father around. Do not wait for the banns to be cried or go to the expense of procuring a special license. Just make a run for the border—of Scotland, that is, where the marriage laws are lenient and you can do away with the formalities of preparing for the ceremony.

1. **Tell no one.** Do not disclose your secret to your maid, your sisters, or even your most particular friends—they no doubt will carry a tale to your parents. Even if they keep your secret, having concealed it might get them in trouble after you reveal your new situation.

2. **Arrange transportation.** If he tries to make you elope on the stage or the mail coach, you might want to rethink the whole idea. After all, if he's too cheap or broke to hire a chaise for your wedding transportation, he will not make much of a husband.

3. **Write a note explaining everything.** Once your parents understand that your darling truly loves you, they will accept the inevitable and prepare to receive their new son. Hide the note well enough that, by the time it is found, you will have a head start if they take a notion to try to prevent the wedding.

4. **Pack light and travel fast.** If your parents do follow you, it is best to move as quickly as possible and get it over with before they can interfere. You will not be gone long; you do not need a lot of luggage.

5. **Do not annoy your fiancé during the trip.** If you ask him stupid questions such as, "Darling, would you still love me if I did not have a fortune of fifty thousand pounds?" you may not like the answer that you receive.

6. **Travel straight through to Gretna Green.** This is the best place to go, as the town is accustomed to situations such as yours. Do not stay over anywhere on your way north; you do not want unkind gossip about how you were "living together" before your marriage.

7. **Find the blacksmith's shop.** The blacksmith in Gretna Green will have performed many marriage ceremonies; for a fee, he will arrange for witnesses and anything else you might need.

8. **Have a contingency plan.** You can depend upon the professionals at Gretna Green; they will provide you with a bed if your parents arrive before the ceremony is complete. Get into the bed with your husband—if your father thinks you are already married and it is too late, he will go away, and you can finish the ceremony.

9. **Take care of the paperwork.** Get the marriage certificate and keep it so you'll have proof that the marriage actually took place.

10. **Go home in triumph.** You have his ring on your finger, and nothing else matters! Be sure to show it off to your neighbors and anyone of your acquaintance that you meet along the way. If they gossip about the disgraceful nature of your marriage, they are just jealous cats.

MARRIAGE OVER THE ANVIL

In 1753, England established a Marriage Act that laid out strict rules: Each party must be twenty-one years old or have the consent of their parents, the marriage banns must have been published over several weeks in each party's parish or a special license obtained from Doctor's Commons, and the wedding must take place in a church before noon with the event noted in the parish records. Marriages contracted in England under other circumstances were subject to annulment. The point of the Act was to throw difficulties in the way of fortune-hunters trying to sweep an heiress into an ill-considered marriage. Obtaining a special license was not difficult, but it was expensive, and many couples in a hurry simply ran away to Scotland.

Scotland's marriage laws were much like England's had been prior to the establishment of the Marriage Act, allowing boys of 14 and girls of 12 to marry without parental consent or church interference. The parties needed only to declare themselves husband and wife before witnesses. Because marriages legally contracted in Scotland were legally binding in England, Scottish villages close to the border established a cottage industry in providing the means for couples to quickly marry. The best-known of these villages was Gretna Green, located just a mile from the Scottish border. Many weddings were held in the romantic confines of the blacksmith's shop, as he was the tradesman of most importance in the town. The more romantic opined that the blacksmith's art, melding different metals together into a new whole, is a metaphor for marriage. Such ceremonies were often referred to as "marriage over the anvil," with professional witnesses hired for the occasion. The tradition continues, and the wedding industry is still thriving in Gretna Green in the twenty-first century.

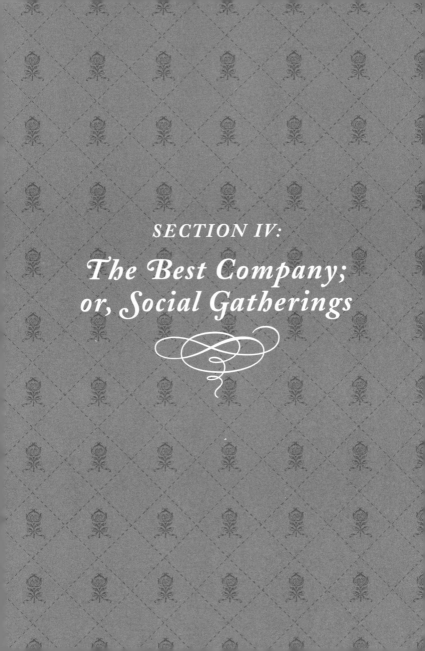

SECTION IV:

*The Best Company;
or, Social Gatherings*

PAY A MORNING CALL

"I made the best excuses I could for not having been able to wait on him and Mrs. Elton on this happy occasion; I said that I hoped I should in the course of the summer. But I ought to have gone before. Not to wait upon a bride is very remiss. Ah! it shews what a sad invalid I am! But I do not like the corner into Vicarage Lane." —MR. WOODHOUSE IN *EMMA*

Morning calls are actually paid between eleven in the morning and three in the afternoon, "morning" being the term used for the time between rising and eating dinner. Do not call any earlier, for a lady might be eating breakfast or busy with household duties; any later than three might make her think you are trying to cadge a dinner invitation.

❦ **Provide yourself with calling cards.** If no one is at home, you can leave your card to show your regard and attention to the person on whom you called, even if you did not get to see her.

❦ **Determine if the person on whom you wish to call is "at home" on that day.** Most people do not stand upon such ceremony, but there are some snobs who like to make others dance attendance on their schedule. If it is not her "at home" day, and you pay a call and leave your card, it looks as though you did not wish to actually meet with that person. It would be better to wait for the proper day.

❦ **Present your card to the butler.** He will ascertain if Madam is at home, or admit you immediately if she is receiving.

◉ **Make pleasant conversation.** If you are not well acquainted with this person, you might not have much to talk about. If this is the case, confine your subjects to the weather and the state of the roads. If the person on whom you are calling has children, they provide an excellent subject. Everyone likes to have their children admired.

◉ **Accept tea or food if it is offered.** A good hostess will offer tea or food such as fruit, cake, or sandwiches to her guests. If conversation is lacking, such an offer can be a godsend: Even if one cannot talk, one can eat.

🌀 **Bring something to keep your hands busy.** If you are paying a call on one of your particular friends, bring along your workbag. An hour or two of chatter and fancy work is a very pleasant way to spend an afternoon. Do not initiate such activity if you are not well-acquainted with the person, but if she pulls out her work, feel free to bring out your own. Your respective projects might be a good subject to bond over.

🌀 **Stay for the proper time.** A formal morning call lasts from a quarter of an hour to half an hour. You may stay longer if you are particular friends with the person upon whom you are calling.

🌀 **Prepare to receive the return call.** Politeness demands that the person upon whom you called will return the call, so expect to see her within a few days. If she does not call, assume that she does not wish to continue the acquaintance.

THE ETIQUETTE OF THE CALLING CARD

🌀 **Keep your card simple.** Calling cards are useful items, for they provide a way to identify oneself and provide vital information to one's acquaintances. Your cards will have your name and, if applicable, the days that you are "at home" to receive callers. Plain black script on a fine white card, perhaps with a simple border, is proper and elegant.

🌀 **When you arrive in town, leave cards at the homes of each of your acquaintances.** Your card will act as an announcement of your arrival and your readiness for receiving callers.

- **Do not leave your card for a gentleman.** A gentleman may leave his card for a lady, or more properly, for her parents or chaperones, but it is improper for an unmarried woman to leave her card for an unmarried man.

- **Pay calls when they are required.** Leave your card or pay a formal call after you are invited to dinner or a party at someone's house, when someone is new to the neighborhood, to visit a newly married bride, and when there is a death in someone's family. Gentlemen should call on their dancing partners the day after a ball.

- **When you pay a call, present your card to the butler.** He will admit you and place the card in a dish or bowl near the door.

- **If you are arriving for a dinner party or ball, place the card in the bowl yourself.**

- **If a person of high rank calls upon you, subtly leave their card where it may be seen by others.** Do not make it seem as though you are displaying the card on purpose. Looking through the cards at other people's houses is somewhat unbecoming, but everyone does it—that's why you leave them out!

BEHAVE AT A DINNER PARTY

Mr. Collins was carefully instructing them in what they were to expect, that the sight of such rooms, so many servants, and so splendid a dinner might not wholly overpower them. —PRIDE AND PREJUDICE

Family meals generally consist of only a few dishes, but formal dinner parties tend to be elaborate affairs, with at least two courses plus dessert. The table will be laid with a tremendous amount of food; the cuisine offered might include several cuts of meat, poultry, fish, pies, vegetables, puddings, "made dishes" or ragouts (dishes combining several foods, baked or stewed with sauce), and even sweet fare such as custards or trifle. And you can eat with your fingers!

GOING IN TO DINNER

1. **The host and hostess will escort the highest-ranking guest of the opposite sex into the dining room.**

2. **Allow those of higher rank to go in ahead of you.** New brides are also given precedence for a few months after their marriage. Truly genteel persons will not insist on the observance of strict precedence, but there always will be a pill who will make a fuss over having his or her rank respected. Surreptitiously complain about him or her to the other guests.

3. **Sit at the table according to rank.** The host and hostess will sit together at the higher end of the table, or one at either

142

end, and will invite the highest-ranking guests to sit next to them. The other guests will take their places accordingly. With a little luck and contrivance, you might be seated next to the object of your desire.

THE MEAL

1. **Help yourself to the dishes within easy reach, and offer to serve some to your neighbors.** The food will be served *à la française*, with the dishes placed on the table for guests to serve themselves. You are not expected to try every dish. If you want soup, ask for it right away, as it will be served and then immediately removed and replaced with another dish.

2. **If you would like to try something out of your reach, pass your plate to the person sitting nearest that dish, or send the servant round with your plate.** You might be eating with your fingers, but the "boardinghouse reach" is still considered inappropriate.

3. **Gentlemen will carve meat placed near them and offer to help their neighbors to a slice.** This is an excellent opportunity for flirtation. An "accidental" touch of the hand can say volumes.

4. **Use your fingers to help cut and eat your food, particularly for tearing apart meat and fowl.** This is perfectly polite behavior. To clean your fingers, dip them into your finger bowl and wipe them discreetly on your napkin or on the part of the tablecloth in your lap. Don't worry about dirtying the cloth, as it will be replaced before the second course and is meant to catch spills and dirt rather than as a decorative item. Don't drink the water in your fingerbowl, but you *can* use it to rinse out your mouth.

5. **Do not overeat!** Try a little bit of several things, and pace yourself for the second course and dessert. Those who show too much interest in their food or are overly finicky about it open themselves to contempt.

6. **Converse brilliantly.** (The men notice that, you know.) Depending on the size of the party, conversation might be general or confined to the persons seated nearest to you. Do not gossip or discuss private business when the servants are present and might overhear and carry gossip below stairs.

7. **Sit quietly while the table is cleared and the second course is laid out.** Do not attempt to converse, as it will be an awkward business with the servants ducking around you. A good hostess will ensure that her servants perform this task quickly so that guests are not unduly inconvenienced. The second course will consist of lighter dishes, though still a great variety. The same guidelines explained above for serving yourself and eating apply.

8. **Save room for syllabub.** The tablecloth will be removed entirely after the second course and the servants will withdraw once the dessert is laid out, permitting more private conversation. The dessert selection might include fruit, jellies, creams, cakes, custards, trifle, syllabub (a sort of Georgian smoothie), cheese and nuts, as well as sweet dessert wine. Candied or jellied fruit is likely to be served, but chocolate candy will not be invented for several decades, so do not expect bon-bons—*quel dommage!*

"DRINKING TEA" & POSTDINNER ENTERTAINMENT

1. **Follow the hostess to the dining room.** When the guests are finished with their dessert, the hostess will rise. The ladies will retire to the drawing room for conversation, reading,

gossip, and needlework until the gentlemen deign to join them, usually thirty minutes to an hour later. If you are hoping to spend time with a particular gentleman, this time will pass very slowly, so read Shakespeare's sonnets or Byron's poetry to properly reflect your tortured state of mind.

2. **When all the gentlemen have returned to the drawing room, offer to help the young ladies of the house pour out the coffee and tea.** Pouring beverages offers an excellent opportunity for a bit of conversation with a certain gentleman. If he brings back his cup for more, assume he is interested.

MEANWHILE, BACK IN THE DINING ROOM . . .

The host will produce a decanter of port, pour a glass, and pass the bottle to the next gentleman, who will pour himself a glass and pass it quickly; it is considered rude to hold up the bottle. Port is always passed to the left—the port side. They might smoke cigars, as no man of breeding would smoke in front of a lady, and perhaps take advantage of a chamber pot hidden in a sideboard. They will drink toasts to the king, to the success of whatever military campaigns are currently going on, and to the lady of their fancy. Conversation will focus on appropriately masculine topics, such as hunting and risqué jokes.

3. **Upon their arrival, greet the guests who were invited only to "drink tea" rather than to dine.** Try to not act superior to those considered by the hostess as good enough company while drinking tea but not while eating dinner.

4. **If you are asked to play the pianoforte, do not linger at the instrument.** Play one or two songs, modestly disclaim your talent, mention something about a sore throat, and let the other young ladies have time to exhibit.

5. **Assist the hostess in making up a card table.** Whist requires four players per game, so if a table is short, offer to sit in— especially if the gentleman in whom you are interested is sitting there.

6. **If you would like to gamble, determine if you can afford the game before sitting down.** Ascertain if they will be "playing high," or for high stakes. Gambling debts are called "debts of honor" and failure to repay them might render one unwelcome in polite society.

7. **Drop a hint in the hostess's ear to roll back the carpet for an impromptu dance.** If you are asked to dance by an undesirable partner, remember that if you decline, you cannot dance with any other gentleman that evening. However, there will most likely be only a few dances, so you will be stuck with the undesirable partner all night anyway. It is perfectly polite to say, "Thank you, I do not care to dance tonight," and spend the night conversing, reading, creating fancy needlework, or pining romantically for the true object of your affection. Try not to get roped into playing for others to dance, as this will mark you as a spinster past all hope.

TAKING WINE

During a meal, someone might catch your eye or say, "May I take wine with you?" and raise their glass. This is a sort of mini toast called "taking wine" and can be a sign of regard, affection, or friendship, or an attempt to curry favor. Simply raise your glass in return and take a sip. Have a care: Taking wine indiscriminately can send the wrong message or lead to intoxication and further regrettable behavior.

PLAY AT CARDS

CAPTAIN WENTWORTH: *"You have not been long enough in Bath,"* said he, *"to enjoy the evening parties of the place."*
ANNE ELLIOT: *"Oh! no. The usual character of them has nothing for me. I am no card-player."*
CAPTAIN WENTWORTH: *"You were not formerly, I know. You did not use to like cards; but time makes many changes."*
—*PERSUASION*

A table or room set aside for card players is almost inevitable at any social gathering. Indeed, some parties are held for no other reason. Nearly everyone plays cards, though context often determines how enjoyable a game will be. Lively games with charming partners are enjoyable pastimes, while parties with no purpose other than making up whist tables with dull company are to be abhorred. In any event, everyone plays cards at some point, so it is best to familiarize yourself with the rules of some of the most popular games.

WHIST
Whist is related to the modern game of bridge.

REQUIREMENTS: Four players and a standard deck of fifty-two cards.

1. **Divide the players into two sets of two partners.** Each player should sit across from his or her partner at the table.

2. **Shuffle and deal all of the cards.** Each player should have thirteen cards. The last card is left turned up; the suit of that card is the trump suit.

3. **Lead the trick.** The player sitting to the left of the dealer "leads" the trick by choosing a card to play from his or her hand.

4. **Play the cards in a clockwise rotation.** Try to play a card of the trump suit but a higher number. If you have none, then you may play a card of any suit.

5. **Take the trick.** The player with the highest card in the trump suit wins the trick. If there is no card from the trump suit, then the highest card from the lead suit wins the trick. When you win a trick, take up the four cards and stack them in front of you.

6. **Pay attention to the cards already played.** If you are attentive, you will know which cards already have been played and can guess your opponents' cards with a fair degree of accuracy. Guessing your opponents' cards is considered part of the strategy of the game.

7. **Count points.** Once a team has won six tricks, they begin to tally points: one point for each trick won.

8. **Deal the cards again.** The game continues until one set of partners wins five points. You will most likely have to deal the cards more than once.

9. **Collect your winnings.** The losers will pay a predetermined amount per point; for instance, if you have decided to play for a pound per point, the losers will each pay five pounds, which is split between the winners.

VINGT-ET-UN

In modern vernacular, this game is known as blackjack.

REQUIREMENTS: Two or more players, a standard deck of fifty-two cards, and fish (fish-shaped betting chips) which may or may not be a substitute for money.

1. **Determine the banker.** Cut the cards; the player with the high card is the banker.

2. **Deal the first card.** The banker deals one card face down to each player.

3. **Make your bid.** Peek at the card you have been dealt and place a bid based on your confidence in reaching a total value of twenty-one when the banker gives you another card. Number cards are worth the number that appears on the card. Face cards, or "court" cards, are valued as follows: Ace = 1, Jack = 11, Queen = 12, King = 13.

4. **Deal the second card face down.** Look at your card and determine how close you are to reaching twenty-one. If the banker already has twenty-one at this point, the game is over, and he or she wins the pot.

5. **Get more cards if you need them.** The banker will ask if you wish to buy a card. If the total value of your cards is still low enough that you want to add more cards to get closer to twenty-one, put an additional bid into the pot. Repeat this until you get as many cards as you need. If the value of your cards is more than twenty-one, you must drop out and lose your stake.

6. **Determine the winner.** When everyone playing is satisfied with the value of their cards, flip them over. The player

whose cards total the closest to twenty-one without going over wins the pot.

SPECULATION

Speculation is a high-spirited game, and players must sharpen their avarice and harden their hearts even against their loved ones to carry it off creditably.

REQUIREMENTS: Two or more players, a standard deck of fifty-two cards, and fish for betting or purchasing cards.

1. **Distribute the fish.** Each player should receive an equal amount of fish.

2. **Ante up.** The dealer antes six fish and the other players four fish each.

3. **Deal each player three cards.**

4. **Determine the trump suit.** The dealer should turn over the next undealt card; the suit of that card is the trump suit.

5. **Play the first round.** The dealer turns over his first card. If it is an ace of the trump suit, the game is over and the dealer wins the pot. If it is not an ace, the dealer may sell or auction the card to any other player, using your fish for payment. The next player then turns over one of his or her cards and decides to keep or sell it. This is repeated until all the cards originally dealt are revealed.

6. **Determine the winner.** The person in possession of the highest card of the trump suit, whether it had been dealt to that player or purchased, wins the pot.

7. **Strategize carefully.** Do not use up all your fish by buying cards, or you may win hands but lose the game.

PIQUET

This game bears many striking similarities to the modern game of poker.

REQUIREMENTS: Two players and a deck of thirty-two cards (a standard deck with the 2 through 6 cards in each suit removed).

1. **Deal the cards.** Twelve cards are dealt to each player, with the eight left over cards, called the "talon," placed face-down in the middle of the table.

2. **Exchange cards.** The nondealer must discard at least one card and may discard up to five cards face down, taking new cards from the top of the talon to replace them. The dealer then discards at least one card and can discard up to however many are left in the talon, also face down. Keep your discards with you, and you may refer to them during the game to see which cards you already have discarded.

3. **Determine if you have carte blanche.** If your hand contains no court cards, declare carte blanche and receive ten points immediately. Announce that you have carte blanche after your opponent has discarded but before you have discarded your own cards, as you must show all of your cards to prove your claim. If you are the nondealer, announce carte blanche and tell your opponent how many cards you plan to discard but do not show your cards. Once she has discarded her own cards, then show your dealt hand to prove that you have carte blanche.

4. **Add your points.** There are three ways to arrive at your score combination; take the combination that provides the highest score for you.

   • *Points.* One point is awarded for each card of a particular suit in your hand; for instance, if you have four hearts, you score four points, no matter which cards make up the grouping. Take this option if you have several high-numbered cards in the same suit, or if you are unable to accrue points in either of the other potential combinations.

   • *Sequence.* Three or four cards in sequence within the same suit scores one point per card; five to eight cards in sequence within the same suit scores one point for each card plus ten more total.

   • *Set.* Three or four of the same court cards or aces. Three cards in a set scores one point each, and four in a set scores one point each plus ten, or fourteen points total.

OTHER CARD GAMES

Quadrille: A popular game in the eighteenth century, quadrille is favored by older people in Jane Austen's novels; Lady Catherine de Bourgh, Mrs. Bates, and Mr. Woodhouse are some of the characters who play quadrille. It is a round game of four players, similar to whist, played with a deck of forty cards and many arcane rules. Trump cards are always the same rather than changing game by game, and players bid or pass on each trick based on their current hand.

Loo: Similar to whist, but with a flexible number of players. The stakes tended to be higher, as one bid and rebid for each trick in which one participated. In gambling halls, the stakes could be ruinous, but at country house parties loo was mostly harmless.

Cribbage: Fanny Price and her aunt Bertram play cribbage in *Mansfield Park*, presumably the five-card variety rather than the six-card cribbage that is played today. Each player is dealt five cards, and a score is determined by combinations of the cards in their hand or those discarded during the play, called the "crib." The tally of points is recorded on a special pegboard, and the first player to reach 61 points (over several hands) wins.

ATTEND A BALL

*It may be possible to do without dancing entirely. Instances
have been known of young people passing many, many months
successively, without being at any ball of any description,
and no material injury accrue either to body or mind;—but
when a beginning is made—when the felicities of rapid
motion have once been, though slightly, felt—it must be a
very heavy set that does not ask for more. —EMMA*

Whether at an elegant ball at a grand house, a village assembly, or in the drawing room after dinner, dancing plays a vital role in the Regency social scene. It is practically the only acceptable way for unmarried ladies and gentlemen to spend time together, and not only is it an enjoyable activity, but it is a way to display one's good breeding and respect for neighbors and fellow dancers. Here are the particulars that will allow you to dance with confidence and grace.

HOW TO PREPARE FOR A BALL

1. **Learn the basic dance steps.** Hire a dancing master to instruct you not only in the intricate steps of dances such as the country dance and quadrille, but also in dance floor etiquette. Study books such as Thompson's or Rutherford's annual collections. For each particular dance, you will need to know the following:
   - *Steps:* The actual footwork you perform during the dance.
   - *Formations:* The location at which you begin and end the dance relative to your partner and the other couples.
   - *Figures:* How you move around the floor during the course of a dance.

2. **Practice.** Dance at home with your sisters or your close friends. Take turns playing the pianoforte for one another, or ask your mother or governess to assist.

3. **Indicate your attendance.** Public assemblies usually require the payment of a fee, which your father will remit on your behalf. If you will be attending a series of balls at the same establishment, your father can obtain a subscription allowing you to attend for the season. For private balls, you will receive a handwritten invitation from the host or hostess, to which you must respond with your acceptance or regrets.

4. **Rest.** On the day of the party, allow yourself to sleep in a bit in the morning, or take a short nap in the afternoon before dinner. If you are not accustomed to dancing until five in the morning, you will be thankful you prepared as the ball proceeds.

5. **Eat lightly.** You do not want to be lethargic when it is time to dance—though you will most likely be too excited to eat much anyway.

6. **Get dressed for the big night.** Dressing for a ball is part of the fun, though it can be a matter for particular concern as well—the gentlemen must ask you to dance, so you will want to look your best. White muslin is always an appropriate and fashionable choice for a young lady, adorned with a simple cross pendant on a gold chain, or perhaps pearls inherited from your mother. Pin back your hair with beads, flowers, or feathers woven through (see "How to Dress," page 91), but allow a few curls to fall around your face.

HOW TO BEHAVE AT A BALL

1. **Pin up your train.** If your gown has a train, pin it up, or gentlemen will assume that you do not wish to dance. Ask your mother, sister, or particular friend to assist, and return the favor for them if needed.

2. **Refuse strangers.** At a public assembly, if a brash fellow with whom you are not acquainted asks you to dance, you must turn him down, however handsome he might be. Propriety demands that he seek an introduction from the master of ceremonies or a mutual acquaintance before he requests your company in a dance. However, at private balls, no introductions are required.

3. **Dance only with gentlemen.** Two ladies (or two gentlemen) should not stand up together unless one sex is greatly outnumbered, and even then permission should be procured from the master of ceremonies.

4. **Take your place in the set.** "Set" refers to the group of dancers participating in a country dance, as well as the actual dance that they perform. Line up in two long lines facing one another, with ladies on one side and gentlemen on the other.

5. **Perform the dance that is called.** The leader for a particular dance will decide the dance to be performed. Do not object to or attempt to change the dance. If you do not like the dance, you may sit down, but sitting down before the dance is completed is a breach of etiquette in itself. You will get a turn at leading the dance eventually, so be a good sport and go along with the crowd.

6. **Maintain your complacence.** Serenity of countenance, elegant carriage, good posture, and graceful movements show your

respect for your company—both your fellow dancers and those watching the dance. Clapping, shouting, snapping your fingers, or other loud interruptions will mark you as vulgar and unaccustomed to good company.

COMING OUT

There was no set way for a young lady to make her debut in society. Her parents or guardians might hold a ball in her honor, as Sir Thomas and Lady Bertram did for Fanny Price in *Mansfield Park*, or she might start attending dinners and evening parties with her parents. In many families it was common for the eldest daughter to at least be engaged before the younger daughters were allowed to come out, presumably so they would not compete with her for potential husbands or embarrass her by becoming engaged first. In *Pride and Prejudice*, Lady Catherine de Bourgh is shocked to learn that Elizabeth Bennet's younger sisters are out before the elder are married. A girl not yet out was expected to be quieter and more demurely dressed than her elder sisters—some, like Mary Crawford in *Mansfield Park*, even felt a girl not yet out should be under the care of her governess rather than making a show of herself in public.

7. **Lead a dance if you are asked.** New brides, a young lady just coming out, or a particularly honored guest might be asked to lead the first dance of a private ball (referred to as "opening the ball"). At public assemblies, the master of ceremonies often will distribute numbered tickets to each lady. Before each dance, he will call out a number, and the lady with the matching ticket will lead the dance. See "How to Lead a Dance" below for details on how to perform this role.

8. **Remain with the same partner for two consecutive dances.** If he asks you again, unless it is a very small ball, take that as a hint that he likes you.

9. **Be polite to your supper partner.** The gentleman with whom you are dancing just before supper will sit with you while you are eating. At a public assembly, he will most likely fetch your tea things. Converse with him pleasantly. An especially clever young lady will contrive to have the most pleasant supper partner possible, though this is an advanced feat of timing.

10. **Thank your hostess.** Send her a note of thanks on the day after the ball to compliment her arrangements and thank her for her hospitality.

HOW TO LEAD A DANCE

If you are asked to lead a dance, you will choose the figure that everyone will follow. This is an opportunity to make the dance fun for everyone, so be prepared.

1. **Request your favorite tune.** The master of ceremonies is likely to oblige, though he might have something in mind already. If that is the case, acquiesce gracefully.

2. **Choose the figures.** Inform the master of ceremonies of which figures you will be dancing so that he might inform the other sets of dancers. Do not make the figures too difficult, especially if there are younger dancers in the group. If the master of ceremonies objects on the grounds of difficulty, choose something easier. Be sure to choose figures that will go with the music; to do otherwise is extremely inappropriate and shows disrespect for your company.

3. **Take your place at the top of the set with your partner.** Everyone's eyes are on you, so stand up straight and smile.

4. **Set the figures.** Weave between the second and third couples in line, dancing the figures you have chosen, ending below the second couple so they are at the top of the set. They then will repeat the figures with the third and fourth couples in the set, ending up below the fourth couple. It will then be your turn to dance again. Continue working your way down the set until you reach the bottom, where you will likely be inactive for a turn.

5. **Support the active dancers.** When you and your partner are inactive, maintain your attention to show your respect for those whose turn it is to move.

6. **Work your way back up the set.** Interact once again with all the couples in the line. Once you have danced to the bottom of the set, to the top again, and then past the next three couples, the dance is finished.

7. **Retire gracefully.** Once your dance is over, take your place at the bottom of the set for the next dance, and let someone else have the privilege of leading the dance.

TYPES OF DANCES

Minuet: Most eighteenth-century dances opened with a minuet, in which each couple took a turn displaying the slow, elegant steps while everyone else watched. By the early nineteenth century, the practice of opening a ball with a minuet became increasingly unpopular because it took too long for all the couples to have a turn, especially at large gatherings.

Cotillion: This dance was similar to modern square dancing. Four couples faced one another in a square formation, dancing successive "changes" followed by a figure that characterized a particular cotillion. Cotillions were considered out of fashion by 1800.

Quadrille: A dance for four couples, in a square formation; each figure had its own distinctive music, with a pause between. Quadrilles became popular in the late Regency.

Country Dance, or Contredanse: A minimum of five couples lined up facing one another in a "set," with gentlemen on one side and ladies on the other. The lead couple danced with the second and third couples in the set, then with the next two couples, then the next two. As they moved down the line, the couple at the top of the line started working their way down, and so on.

Reel: A Scottish dance in which four dancers performed figures that wove in and out of one another; the music would pause, and they did fancy footwork similar to a Highland fling. Reels became popular after the Prince of Wales visited Edinburgh in 1801.

ᴀVOID ᴅANCING ᴡITH ᴀN UNDESIRABLE ᴘARTNER

Every young lady may feel for my heroine in this critical moment, for every young lady has at some time or other known the same agitation. All have been, or at least all have believed themselves to be, in danger from the pursuit of some one whom they wished to avoid; and all have been anxious for the attentions of someone whom they wished to please. —NORTHANGER ABBEY

At a ball, when you wish to avoid dancing with a particular gentleman who makes it clear he is determined to be your partner, the difficulty is not in refusing him, for that is your right; the difficulty is in retaining your right to dance with another gentleman afterwards. If you refuse one partner, politeness calls for you to refuse all of them. Careful planning and the use of avoidance techniques will free you from this uncomfortable situation.

◉ **Avoid him.** Stay away from him early in the evening. Employ your girlfriends to help you. With luck, other gentlemen will ask you for all the available dances.

◉ **Take advantage of the noise of a ballroom.** Pretend to not hear him when he asks you to dance.

◉ **Hide from him.** It is undignified, but if he cannot see you, he cannot ask you to dance.

◉ **Lie.** Tell him that these dances are promised to someone

else. However, if you do so but do not have a partner, you will have to sit the dances out, so this is not the best choice—nor is it the most graceful.

❀ **Accept the inevitable.** Just get it over with, especially if it looks like no one else is going to ask you for those two dances anyway. When they are over, excuse yourself gracefully.

❀ **Let him know that you are not interested in him.** If you must dance with him, do not put yourself out to be charming. Remarks on the weather or the state of the roads are sufficient. You need not please him; in fact, if you insult him, he most likely will not ask you again.

◎ **Appeal to his sense of honor.** If, after you've already danced with him, he pesters you to dance again, tell him that you fear for your reputation if you appear too particular. If he continues to press you, drop hints that you will tell everyone that his manners are not what they should be.

THE FORBIDDEN DANCE: THE WALTZ

Hot from the hands promiscuously applied
Round the slight waist, or down the glowing side.
—LORD BYRON, "THE WALTZ"

The waltz was not commonly danced in England during Jane Austen's lifetime. Military officers brought knowledge of the dance home with them when they returned to England from the Continent after the Napoleonic Wars (1803–15). No other dance had ever been seen in which couples danced face to face; British society was shocked at the idea of couples on the dance floor in a near-embrace, especially unmarried couples, and waltzing was slow to catch on except in the most fashionable circles. Jane Austen mentions waltzes in *Emma*, but since Frank Churchill "secured (Emma's) hand, and led her up to the top," most likely it was a country dance performed to music in waltz time, which was a socially acceptable compromise.

CONVERSE WITH YOUR DANCING PARTNER

*"It is your turn to say something now, Mr. Darcy. —
I talked about the dance, and you ought to make some
kind of remark on the size of the room, or the number
of couples." He smiled, and assured her that whatever
she wished him to say should be said.* —ELIZABETH
BENNET AND MR. DARCY IN *PRIDE AND PREJUDICE*

A very wise man once compared a country dance to marriage.
He might have been stretching his metaphor a bit, but one point
is well-taken: You have your partner's undivided attention for an
hour or so. A smart girl takes advantage of this time by having
an intelligent and witty conversation with her partner.

🎵 **Talk about what interests him.** This might seem obvious,
but more than one young lady has bored her partner by nat-
tering on about muslins or something equally silly. If he is
any kind of a gentleman, he will at least pretend to be interested in the subject, so do be aware of what you are saying.

🎵 **Tease him.** He will pretend to not understand you, or to be
offended, but deep down he enjoys it.

🎵 **Make him laugh.** Even if you did not intend to be funny,
you will endear yourself to him.

🎵 **Praise his good deeds.** If he danced with a young lady in
need of a partner, saving her from humiliation, let him
know that you noticed and that you approve.

THE DEMOCRACY OF THE DANCE

In the eighteenth century and earlier, the most fashionable dancing was in the French style, particularly the minuet, which was danced by one couple at a time with everyone else watching. The idea of the minuet was to perform gracefully and give enjoyment to those watching. The highest-ranking persons would dance together, and so on down the line, so the social order was strictly observed.

English country dancing, which came into prominence on both sides of the English Channel after the French Revolution, was a more democratic style of dancing. As a couple worked their way down the set, they interacted with every other couple in the set. Aristocrats would interact with gentry, tradespeople, or even servants who were called in to make up a set if there were not enough couples, giving them their hands and looking them in the eye. Those who considered themselves "above their company," such as Mr. Darcy at the Meryton assembly in *Pride and Prejudice*, greatly insulted those present.

◉ **Play hard to get.** Many men like a challenge, so do not make it too easy for him to hold your attention. Talk to your girlfriends or even other gentlemen. But be careful! In such a case, some men will redouble their efforts to impress you, but some will give you up as a bad prospect. Use this skill judiciously.

◉ **Be prepared for silence.** Sometimes his mood might call for just that.

GET AN INVITATION TO A COUNTRY HOUSE PARTY

Northanger Abbey! — These were thrilling words, and wound up Catherine's feelings to the highest point of exstasy. Her grateful and gratified heart could hardly restrain its expressions within the language of tolerable calmness. To receive so flattering an invitation! To have her company so warmly solicited! Everything honourable and soothing, every present enjoyment, and every future hope was contained in it; and her acceptance, with only the saving clause of Papa and Mamma's approbation, was eagerly given. —NORTHANGER ABBEY

Even if you live in a grand estate, everyone likes to get away from time to time for a change of scenery. A house party can be the very thing: There will be new scenes and new people; you will have company, so you will not be bored; and as it is not your house, you have no business to take care of. And if your pockets are all to let, a stay of a few weeks will give you the opportunity to catch up with your debts. Here are some tips for securing yourself an invitation.

❧ **Cultivate relationships with people who have big houses.** They will want to gather company around them, and you are bound to get an invitation sooner or later.

❧ **Offer to keep house for a bachelor relative.** A gentleman cannot invite ladies to his home for dinner or a ball unless there is a lady to receive them, so if a bachelor brother or other close relative would like to extend hospitality to his neighbors, he will be happy to have you keep house for him.

This does take some of the fun out of it for you, since you will have to consult with the housekeeper and take care of the little details. While you are there, look around for a wife for him; when he gets married, he is sure to invite you back, and you can relax and enjoy yourself while his wife takes care of the house.

🏵 **Make yourself invaluable.** Offer advice or lend money; whatever the owner of the house might need. He will be so grateful that you are sure to be invited. Help with a romance, and the happy couple will always be glad to invite you to stay with them. Listen to the owners' problems, cheer them when they are feeling ill, and help out with their children.

🏵 **Play the pity card.** Drop hints into your conversation about how country air agrees so well with you, but you are forced by circumstances to stay in the city just at this time. Cultivate an air of brave forbearance. They will trip over themselves to offer you a few weeks in the country.

🏵 **Ask!** Sometimes the direct approach works better than you'd think.

🏵 **Just be good company.** You will have more invitations than you know what to do with.

GET RID OF
UNWANTED GUESTS

*Lydia was occasionally a visitor there, when her husband
was gone to enjoy himself in London or Bath; and with
the Bingleys they both of them frequently staid so long,
that even Bingley's good humour was overcome, and
he proceeded so far as to* talk *of giving them a hint
to be gone.* —**PRIDE AND PREJUDICE**

It has been said that fish and guests stink after three days. You
may be rather more generous than that; a month or six weeks
is not too much for someone whose company you truly enjoy;
and family will usually hang around much longer than they are
really welcome. When you are finally fed up with guests and
want them gone, it can be an uncomfortable situation, but
there are some ways to deal with it.

🌑 **Give them a hint.** Sometimes this is enough, but most of
the time it will just be ignored. If so, you must be prepared
to escalate hostilities.

🌑 **Stop the party.** Do not provide any enjoyable activities. No
balls, no shooting, no amateur theatricals. They will go
elsewhere in search of a good time.

🌑 **Go away yourself.** Come up with an engagement of your
own that takes you away from home. They can hardly expect
to stay if you are not there.

🌑 **Frighten them away.** Tell them that there is a putrid fever in the house. This is especially effective if the guests have children with them.

● **Use a middleman.** Why should you do the dirty work? Get someone else to inform the guest that she must leave in the morning. Order her a chaise and be done with it.

PAYING EXTENDED VISITS

In Jane Austen's time, it was expected that a houseguest would stay a minimum of two weeks. Four to six weeks was a more common length of time, and two months or more was not unheard of. Country dwellers, especially those living in an isolated area, often were happy to have company for an extended period, and considering the difficulty and expense of traveling long distances, it would have been illogical to turn around and go home after only a few days. Unmarried women could not travel alone, and if a servant could not be spared as an escort, they might have to wait until a friend or male relative was available to accompany them home. Modern audiences might marvel at the length of these visits, but recall that everyone had servants to tend to things at home and rarely had a job to which they must return.

CELEBRATE CHRISTMAS
IN A COUNTRY HOUSE

*On one side was a table occupied by some chattering girls,
cutting up silk and gold paper; and on the other were
tressels and trays, bending under the weight of brawn
and cold pies, where riotous boys were holding high revel;
the whole completed by a roaring Christmas fire, which
seemed determined to be heard, in spite of all the noise
of the others.* —PERSUASION

The holiday season stretches from December 21 through
January 6, and families and friends gather to enjoy one another's
company during the darkest days of winter. Here is the schedule
your celebration will follow.

🕎 **December 21, the winter solstice:** If you are the owner of
the house, make sure that the Yule log is brought in at this
time and that the fire is kept roaring throughout the holiday.
Have the servants deck the halls with boughs of holly and
other greenery; in more superstitious households, they do
not put out the greenery until December 24, as it is considered unlucky to do so earlier. This is the shortest day of the
year (in the north of England it is very short indeed) and
you will want these reminders of warmth and life around
you. No Christmas tree, however; they will not become
fashionable until the 1850s.

🕎 **December 24, Christmas Eve:** Gather at the appointed
house; settle in and greet your family and friends. Guests
will likely be invited for dinner, and perhaps some dancing

or games afterwards. Do not stay up too late; it's a long holiday season, and you need to pace yourself.

🌑 **December 25, Christmas Day:** Go to church in the morning, and put a little extra in the poor box for tomorrow. Later in the day, enjoy a turkey dinner (the Christmas goose is a later tradition). Most people will stay at home with their families on Christmas Day, so do not expect a large party after dinner, but you still can have games and other fun activities.

🌑 **December 26, Boxing Day:** Give out boxes of food and clothing to the tenants. It also is traditional to give the servants a holiday bonus. The contents of the church poor box will be distributed to the needy, including your extra contribution from the day before; it is hoped that you were generous! There might be a fox hunt put on somewhere in the neighborhood; take part if that is your thing.

🌑 **December 27–30:** There will be parties and gatherings at home or at nearby houses almost every night. Gentlemen will dance all night and then rise early for sport, but ladies can get their beauty rest and then spend the afternoon touring the countryside in a low phaeton. Evening activities can include games, charades, amateur theatricals, or dancing and music.

🌑 **December 31:** See in the New Year at midnight with drink and song, should auld acquaintance be forgot. If you like, get caught under the mistletoe.

🌑 **January 1:** Recover from the previous night's activities and rest up for more partying.

❧ **January 2–5:** More social gatherings and family activities. If it is cold enough, there might be sleighing or ice skating during the day, and balls and parties in the evening.

❧ **January 6, Twelfth Night:** This is the traditional day for the exchange of gifts, but gifts can be given at any time throughout the holiday season or even over several days. At night there will likely be a large ball somewhere in the neighborhood to which the children of the house might be invited along with the grown-ups.

January 7: Take down the decorations (it is unlucky to leave them up longer) and say goodbye to your guests.

Appendix

A SHORT BIOGRAPHY
OF JANE AUSTEN

*Short and easy will be the task of the mere biographer.
A life of usefulness, literature, and religion, was not by any
means a life of event.* —FROM HENRY AUSTEN'S BIOGRAPHICAL
SKETCH OF HIS SISTER, PUBLISHED POSTHUMOUSLY WITH
NORTHANGER ABBEY AND *PERSUASION*

The image persists of Jane Austen as a prim spinster penning
works of accidental genius in rural retirement, despite the efforts
of some biographers to rescue her from the well-intentioned
protection of two generations of her family. While she preferred to live in the country and did not engage in the literary
society of her day, Jane Austen traveled and read and lived and
loved. Like her books, her life was much more interesting than
first glance reveals.

Jane Austen was born on December 16, 1775, in the village of
Steventon in Hampshire, where her father was the parson. The
seventh of eight children, and the younger of two girls, she showed
an early talent for invention, writing short tales full of broad, vio-
lent humor as early as age twelve. She briefly attended two different girls' boarding schools, but she received most of her education
at home, with her father and brothers directing her reading from
the volumes in the parsonage library. She was not denied "unladylike" material; she mentioned Henry Fielding's bawdy novel *Tom
Jones* in one of her letters and wrote that the Austen family were
"great novel readers and not ashamed of being so." Anne Lefroy,
the wife of the rector of Ashe, a neighboring parish, was a mentor
to young Jane. Madam Lefroy, as she was known, was a well-bred,

educated woman and the social leader of the neighborhood.

Surviving letters show that the 20-year-old Jane enjoyed the usual interests of a young woman: clothes, men, and dancing at balls. She engaged in a brief but apparently intense flirtation with law student Thomas Langlois Lefroy, Madam Lefroy's nephew, in December 1795. Austen biographers disagree on the significance of this romance in Jane's life. In a memoir by her nephew, the romance with Tom Lefroy was dismissed as unimportant except as proof that, like her heroines, Jane had felt the pangs of young love. Later biographers, however, considered it a watershed moment in her life. Lefroy family members recalled that Madam Lefroy sent Tom away, fearing that he had raised expectations in Jane that he had no intention of fulfilling. Tom married an heiress in 1799 and later became lord chief justice of Ireland.

Jane's closest relationship throughout her life was with her sister Cassandra. Mrs. Austen told one of her granddaughters that "if Cassandra's head had been going to be cut off, Jane would have hers cut off too." In 1796, Cassandra's fiancé, Tom Fowle, went to the West Indies as a ship's chaplain and died there of yellow fever. Cassandra took on the dress of a spinster, indicating her disinterest in marrying, and Jane followed her example.

Jane continued writing throughout her teens and early twenties. *Lady Susan*, a remarkable novella in letters with an ambitious and amoral title character, was composed in about 1795, and Jane also began her first full-length work that year, an epistolary novel that she titled *Elinor and Marianne*. The next year, she began another long work, called *First Impressions*. Mr. Austen thought so well of *First Impressions* that he wrote to offer it to the publisher Thomas Cadell; the offer was declined. Jane set to work rewriting *Elinor and Marianne* in narrative form, and in 1798 began a novel she called *Susan*.

In 1801, Mr. Austen retired, and he and his wife and daughters moved to Bath. Legend has it that Jane fainted when she was told of the decision to move. Her letters show that she put on a brave face, but it is generally accepted among Austen scholars that she was unhappy in Bath.

During a visit to her friends Catherine and Alethea Bigg at their father's estate, Manydown Park, in December 1802, Jane received a proposal of marriage from Harris Bigg-Wither, the heir to the estate. Jane was not in love with Harris, nor he with her, but if she accepted him, Jane eventually would become the mistress of Manydown and could offer a home and security to her mother and sister. Jane accepted Harris's proposal, but then rescinded her acceptance the next morning. A few months later, Jane made her first literary sale: the copyright of *Susan* to the publisher Richard Crosby and Son for the princely sum of ten pounds (in modern amounts, about $750).

The Austens traveled to the seaside in the summer, and many years after Jane's death, Cassandra Austen told her niece Caroline Austen that Jane had attracted the admiration of a fine young man on one of these summer trips. He had inquired where they might be spending the next summer, and may have intended to renew the acquaintance and his attentions to Jane, which Cassandra hinted would have been successful. But they later heard the news of the young man's sudden death. His name and the exact date and place of this romance by the sea are unfortunately lost.

In 1804, Jane began a novel that she called *The Watsons*, but she abandoned it around the time of her father's death in 1805. James Austen took over Mr. Austen's position as the rector of Steventon, and, left with very little income, the Austen ladies were in difficult straits. The brothers each chipped in what they could afford for their support; nonetheless, the women were obliged to move several times within Bath in search of affordable lodgings until Francis Austen and his wife offered to share their house in Southampton. Martha Lloyd, one of Jane's closest friends, came to live with them, having been left with no home and little money after the death of her mother. In 1808, Edward Austen offered his mother a cottage in the Hampshire village of Chawton, part of one of the estates that he had inherited from a rich cousin. The ladies eagerly accepted and moved for the final time.

Jane's genius flourished in the tranquil setting of Chawton. Mrs. Austen tended the garden, Cassandra kept house, and Martha oversaw the cooking, freeing Jane to spend most of her time writing. She revised *Elinor and Marianne*, retitling it *Sense and Sensibility*, and it was published by Thomas Egerton in 1811. It was the current custom that if a book did not sell enough copies to cover the expense of publication, the author was responsible for repaying the publisher's losses. Jane put away a little money in anticipation of such an expense, but her concern was unnecessary—the book sold well and received good reviews, and Jane was delighted to receive £140 in royalties (about $12,000 today). All of her novels were published anonymously; *Sense and Sensibility* carried only the information that it was written "by a lady." Many of her family members were unaware of Jane's authorship for several years.

Jane then set about revising *First Impressions*. A book had been published by that title in 1800, so she took a phrase from the final chapter of Fanny Burney's novel *Cecilia* for its title: *Pride and Prejudice*. She "lop't and crop't" the original manuscript, and based on the success of *Sense and Sensibility*, Egerton purchased the copyright for £110 (about $9,000). Jane embarked on the most creative period in her life as she set about working on an entirely new novel, *Mansfield Park*, in 1812, publishing it in 1814. Jane's authorial skills had grown, and in *Mansfield Park* she addressed themes of morality and women's position in society with more ambition and subtlety than in her first two books. She had a falling-out with Egerton

JANE AUSTEN'S IMMEDIATE FAMILY

Rev. George Austen (1731–1805): Jane Austen's father; a graduate of St. John's College, Oxford; the rector of Steventon and Deane. At the parsonage that formed part of his compensation, he farmed the land and also tutored and boarded boys. He was proud of Jane and encouraged her writing, providing her with notebooks and querying a publisher about the novel that would eventually become *Pride and Prejudice*.

Cassandra (Leigh) Austen (1739–1827): Jane's mother, who was proud of her aristocratic lineage but nonetheless dug her own potatoes and darned socks in the presence of morning callers. Like her younger daughter, she was clever with words, writing verses and solving word puzzles.

Rev. James Austen (1765–1819): Another literary Austen, he founded a publication called *The Loiterer* while a student at Oxford and wrote poetry his whole life. James took over the parish of Steventon when his father died. James's son James Edward Austen-Leigh wrote the *Memoir of Jane Austen*.

George Austen (1766–1838): Little is known about George, who was not mentioned in early biographies of his famous sister. George experienced unspecified developmental problems as a child and was sent to live with a family in a neighboring village. It is thought that he might have been deaf, because Jane mentions talking to a deaf man "with (her) fingers" in one of her letters—she might have learned sign language to communicate with George.

Edward Austen, later Edward Knight (1767–1852): Edward was adopted by rich, childless cousins, the Knights, and groomed to be the heir to two estates. After his father's death, he offered his mother and sisters a cottage on one of his estates, Chawton in Hampshire. Edward's grandson Lord Brabourne, the son of Fanny Knight (Lady Knatchbull), was the first to publish a collection of Jane Austen's letters.

Rev. Henry Austen (1771–1850): Henry was educated for the church but instead joined the militia. He became paymaster, which led to a career in banking, and he married his widowed cousin, Eliza de Feuillide, and together they lived a fashionable lifestyle in London. Henry acted as Jane's agent with her publishers, as it was unseemly for a woman to do business on her own behalf. A few years after Eliza's death, Henry's bank failed, and he took holy orders.

Cassandra Austen (1773–1845): Jane's beloved elder sister, closest friend, and confidante. Jane discussed all of her works in progress with Cassandra and appointed her as literary executor. Many Austen scholars are unhappy with Cassandra for burning most of her letters from Jane and editing the remaining letters with scissors, but it is certain that she did so in accordance with Jane's own wishes. Cassandra's reminiscences of Jane were recorded by her nieces and nephews, and her notes about the dates of the novels' composition have proven invaluable to biographers and scholars.

Admiral Sir Francis Austen (1774–1865): Frank Austen went to the Royal Naval Academy at Portsmouth at the age of twelve and had a successful naval career. He was knighted by Queen Victoria and was promoted to Admiral of the Fleet, the highest rank possible in the Royal Navy. He advised Jane on naval matters for *Mansfield Park* and *Persuasion*.

Admiral Charles Austen (1779–1852): Charles was the youngest Austen sibling, Jane and Cassandra's "own particular little brother." He followed Frank into the Royal Navy and achieved the rank of rear admiral. His gift of "topaze" crosses to his sisters inspired the episode of Fanny Price's amber cross, a gift from her naval-officer brother, in *Mansfield Park*.

over the second edition, and her next book, *Emma*, was brought out by John Murray, publisher of Walter Scott and Lord Byron.

The increasing fame of Jane's novels had lessened her anonymity, assisted by her brother Henry: Whenever he heard her novels praised, he proudly revealed the identity of the author, both amusing and exasperating his sister. Frank Austen, a naval officer, pointed out that using the names of some of his former ships in *Mansfield Park* might give away the authoress's identity, and she seemed resigned to her growing fame, though never completely comfortable with it.

While Jane was in London tending to the proofs of *Emma* in 1815, Henry fell ill. One of the physicians who attended him also attended the Prince Regent and informed His Royal Highness, who was an admirer of Jane's novels, that the author of *Pride and Prejudice* was in London. The Prince Regent ordered his librarian, James Stanier Clarke, to wait upon Miss Austen. Mr. Clarke not only showed Jane around the Regent's opulent residence, Carlton House, but offered advice on the type of book she should write—advice that was politely rejected and privately mocked.

In the summer of 1815, Jane began composing her final completed novel, *The Elliots*. Late that year, she began to feel the first symptoms of what would be her fatal illness. Which disease she suffered is not known, though based on details in her letters and from family members, a twentieth-century physician diagnosed it as Addison's disease, an ailment of the adrenal glands that can be secondary to tuberculosis. The symptoms include weakness and fatigue, weight loss, nausea and vomiting, low blood pressure, and vitiligo; today the disease is controlled with cortisone, but at that time there was no cure. Despite her increasing debility, Jane completed *The Elliots* in the summer of 1816 and wrote a few chapters of a new novel that she called *The Brothers*—now known as *Sanditon*—in early 1817, but abandoned work on it in March.

In May, Jane and Cassandra went to Winchester to seek medical advice. Jane did not respond to the treatment and died early in the morning of July 18, 1817. Henry Austen arranged to have her buried in Winchester Cathedral.

Jane left nearly all her small fortune to Cassandra, whom she made her literary executor. John Murray published the two remaining completed manuscripts, which Henry and Cassandra retitled *Northanger Abbey* and *Persuasion*, as a four-volume set in 1818, including a short biographical notice by Henry naming Jane Austen as the author for the first time. Throughout the nineteenth century, she had admirers on both sides of the Atlantic. Before her death in 1845, Cassandra burnt most of her letters from Jane, keeping some that were bequeathed to various nieces and nephews, along with the notebooks containing the stories that Jane wrote as a young girl (known collectively as the juvenilia), *Lady Susan*, and the unfinished works.

In 1870, James Austen's son, James Edward Austen-Leigh, published a memoir of his aunt using letters that still remained in the family's possession and canvassing his sisters and cousins for their memories of Aunt Jane. The memoir is a touching and enjoyable read, and though the author's esteem for his aunt is obvious, it nonetheless set the standard for the Victorian view of Jane Austen as a quiet spinster living a retired life and writing on her "little bit (two inches wide) of ivory." In the 1920s, R. W. Chapman edited and annotated the novels and later the juvenilia and unpublished manuscripts, poetry, and other scraps for publication by Oxford University Press, marking the beginning of modern Austen scholarship.

Today, Jane Austen Societies flourish in the UK, North America, South America, Australia, New Zealand, and Japan, and there is a brisk trade in various editions of the novels, both scholarly and not, as well as fiction inspired by her novels and numerous film and television adaptations. Jane Austen's prominence in pop culture rises and falls, but she is always present. In *Mansfield Park*, she wrote that Shakespeare "is a part of an Englishman's constitution"; today, Jane Austen is herself a cultural icon, and part of the constitution of Janeites everywhere.

JANE AUSTEN'S NOVELS

SENSE AND SENSIBILITY
Working Title: *Elinor and Marianne*
Written: 1795
Revised: 1797 and 1809–10
Published: 1811

Sense and Sensibility presents the stark realities of romance in Jane Austen's time. The complex story is softened with some-times savage humor and a cast of memorable characters.

When their father dies, the Dashwood sisters—sensible Elinor and headstrong, romantic Marianne—are left without much in the way of fortune, uprooting them from the comfortable life they had known and complicating their romantic relationships.

Elinor's lover, Edward Ferrars, is secretly engaged to the vulgar, grasping Lucy Steele, who triumphs over Elinor while not allow-ing her to reveal the secret. Marianne has fallen in love with the dashing Willoughby and behaves in a manner that leads everyone to think that they are engaged. Colonel Brandon, the friend of a neighbor and nearly twenty years older than Marianne, admires her but understands that he doesn't stand a chance.

When Marianne learns that Willoughby is engaged to a rich young lady and will marry her within a few weeks, she is dev-astated and succumbs to her emotions. Her health suffers, and Elinor nurses her while nursing her own heartbreak over Edward; Marianne falls into a decline and nearly dies.

When the secret of Edward's engagement is revealed, his mother disinherits him, ironically freeing him from family constraints that prevent his marriage; fortunately for him, Lucy Steele fixes upon his now-rich younger brother, and Edward and Elinor are free to marry. Marianne recovers her health and learns that fiery passion can flame out, and that steady affection from a true heart, such as Colonel Brandon's, can be equally acceptable even to a romantic.

Sense and Sensibility was originally written as an epistolary novel, but after she finished *Pride and Prejudice*, Jane Austen rewrote *Sense and Sensibility* as a prose novel. The novel was published in 1811, receiving generally favorable reviews praising its good morals and sense, but some readers found it too "natural"—that is, too much like real life—to be a good read. Nonetheless, it sold well and went into a second printing.

PRIDE AND PREJUDICE

Working Title: *First Impressions*
Written: 1796–97
Revised: 1811–12
Published: 1813

Pride and Prejudice is Jane Austen's best-known work; it has been popular since it was first published and is now widely respected. One of the most famous opening lines in literature, "It is a truth universally acknowledged that a single man in possession of a good fortune must be in want of a wife," gets the novel off to a rousing start. The heroine, Elizabeth Bennet, is one of five sisters; her father's estate is entailed on a distant cousin, and her silly, shallow mother is anxious to get the girls married off, a difficult task in the face of their limited fortunes. Mrs. Bennet is delighted when a rich young man, Mr. Bingley, leases a nearby estate, hoping that one of her daughters will take his fancy. Mr. Bingley obliges her by taking an obvious interest in the beautiful eldest daughter, Jane. He has an even richer friend, Mr. Darcy, staying with him, but

Mr. Darcy's arrogant pride disgusts the neighborhood in general and Elizabeth in particular. Nonetheless, Mr. Darcy shows a marked interest in Elizabeth, though he is often the victim of her lively wit.

A series of misunderstandings, marriage proposals, and elopements ensues, with Elizabeth and Mr. Darcy learning to better understand themselves and each other. They become engaged at the end of the book, and the attentive reader knows that it is more than a match between a rich man and a pretty girl: It is a true meeting of minds, hearts, and two complex, complementary personalities.

Pride and Prejudice received excellent reviews and sold well, and Jane herself was rather giddy with the happiness of publication, writing a letter to Cassandra jokingly enumerating how it could be improved: "The work is rather too light, and bright, and sparkling; it wants shade; it wants to be stretched out here and there with a long Chapter of something unconnected with the Story; an essay on Writing, a critique on Walter Scott, or the history of Buonaparte, or anything that would form a contrast, and bring the reader with increased delight to the playfulness and Epigrammatism of the general style." More than one latter-day critic (and at least one film director) has unwisely taken those words seriously, but most readers are delighted with the book exactly as it is—as it seems Jane Austen was herself.

MANSFIELD PARK
Written: 1812–13
Published: 1814

In *Mansfield Park*, Jane Austen explores morality in an almost Darwinian framework, showing how morals and proper decision-making skills can be taught to every child and are not simply bestowed upon those brought up in wealthy houses.

The heroine, Fanny Price, is a humble relation brought up at Mansfield Park, the house of her wealthy uncle, Sir Thomas Bertram. Fanny's cousin Edmund Bertram, destined for the church, is kind to her and directs her reading and education, while her aunts make her a sort of unpaid servant who fetches and carries and acts as a companion.

The social world of the Park is turned upside down with the arrival of Mary and Henry Crawford, the sister and brother of the rector's wife. The Bertram sisters are interested in Henry, and he is in return interested in the eldest daughter, Maria, who is already engaged to a stupid but rich man. Edmund is attracted to Mary Crawford, and confides in Fanny. Fanny is in love with Edmund, and these revelations, and Edmund's rationalization of Mary's moral shortcomings, distress her. Fanny suffers even more when Henry Crawford, having toyed with her cousins' hearts, turns his attention to her. Henry falls in love with Fanny and proposes; Fanny, having witnessed his cruel behavior to her cousins, cannot accept him. Sir Thomas, not understanding Fanny's reticence in the face of such an excellent potential marriage, sends her back to her own family in Portsmouth. The Prices are relatively poor, but Fanny perseveres and her refusal of Henry Crawford is shown to be right when he has an affair with the now-married Maria. Fanny is welcomed back to Mansfield Park and eventually into Edmund's heart as well.

Mansfield Park is considered by many Janeites to be her "problem novel," with its very moral and upright (and sometimes judgmental) hero and heroine; even Cassandra Austen thought that Fanny Price should have married Henry Crawford rather than Edmund. However, Jane followed her instincts and wrote the novel she set out to create, and Janeites have discussed it vigorously and sometimes combatively for nearly two centuries.

EMMA

Written: 1814–15
Published: 1815

Jane Austen feared she had created a heroine "whom nobody but myself will much like" in Emma Woodhouse, but many scholars and rank-and-file Janeites alike consider *Emma* to be Jane Austen's finest novel.

Emma Woodhouse, "handsome, clever, and rich," and only twenty-one years old, is the queen of Highbury. Everyone defers to her—everyone, that is, except her neighbor, Mr. Knightley, the only person who ever criticizes Emma's behavior.

Convinced that her own endeavors brought about a marriage between her former governess and a neighbor, Emma sets out to make another match between the vicar, Mr. Elton, and a young lady of obscure background, Harriet Smith. She learns, to her dismay, that Mr. Elton actually is interested in Emma herself (or in her fortune of thirty thousand pounds). Mr. Elton marries a vulgar social climber from Bristol, who takes an interest in Jane Fairfax, the orphaned granddaughter of the late vicar. Jane has no fortune, but was educated to become a governess, and Mrs. Elton sets out to find her a proper situation.

Mrs. Weston's stepson, Frank Churchill, comes to Highbury, and Emma is interested in him at first but then decides to make a match between Frank and Harriet. Unfortunately for Emma, Harriet has other ideas, revealing that she prefers Mr. Knightley. Emma realizes that Harriet cannot marry Mr. Knightley—indeed, no one can, except Emma herself. Things are sorted out amicably, and the happy couple has only the obstacle of Emma's valetudinarian father to overcome.

James Stanier Clarke, the Prince Regent's librarian, informed Jane that she might dedicate her next work to the Prince Regent without asking any further permission, which Jane realized meant that the Regent expected her to do so. Thus, though she disliked the Regent, Jane directed Murray to add a grudgingly short dedication to *Emma*. Murray informed her that something longer would be proper, and *Emma* bore the fulsome dedication: "To His Royal Highness, the Prince Regent, this work is, by His Royal Highness's permission, most respectfully dedicated, by His Royal Highness's dutiful and obedient humble servant, the Author." The novel was published in December 1815 (though the title page bore the date 1816) and received generally good reviews, including an admiring article by Walter Scott for the important literary journal the *Quarterly Review*.

NORTHANGER ABBEY
Working Title: *Susan*
Written: 1798–1803
Revised: 1816
Published: 1818

Composed when Jane Austen was in her early twenties, *Northanger Abbey* is a bridge between the rollicking humor of the stories Jane wrote as a young girl and her more mature work. It is an affectionately comic parody of the Gothic and sentimental novels popular in her time as well as a coming-of-age story of the naïve but lovable heroine, Catherine Morland. Catherine is not a typical heroine: She is not a prodigy, nor is she accomplished, well-read, or even beautiful, though she can manage "almost pretty" on a good day. Invited to Bath by rich, childless neighbors, she meets Henry Tilney, a young clergyman who amuses her with witty nonsense, and Isabella Thorpe, a fashionable young lady who introduces her to the delights of "horrid" Gothic novels such as Ann Radcliffe's *The Mysteries of Udolpho*.

Isabella's brother John attempts to court Catherine, but she thinks him crude and vulgar and remains interested in Henry Tilney. Catherine's brother James becomes engaged to Isabella, but Isabella distresses Catherine by flirting with Henry's elder brother, the heir of Northanger Abbey. Henry's father, General Tilney, takes an interest in Catherine, and Henry's sister, Eleanor, invites her to the Abbey. There, Catherine's imagination, inspired by horrid novels, takes a morbid turn, and she begins to imagine strange things about the General; Henry disabuses her of these notions, but later, the General shows himself to be little better than the villain that she had imagined. Catherine learns to trust her instincts; namely, that people do not always mean what they say; that real life is not like books, especially of the horrid variety; that a hero can be quite an ordinary fellow; and that villains can be quite dastardly even without committing murder.

Jane Austen sold the copyright of this novel, which she originally called *Susan*, for £10 to Richard Crosby and Son in 1803. Crosby advertised *Susan* for publication but never brought it out. In 1816, once Jane had earned a little money from her books, Henry Austen bought back the manuscript on her behalf. When the transaction was completed, he informed Crosby that the anonymous manuscript was written by the author of the very popular *Pride and Prejudice*. A novel titled *Susan* had been published by someone else in the meantime, so Jane changed the heroine's name to Catherine and wrote a short apologia for details that had become out of date during the thirteen years the novel had languished. She fell ill and did not pursue publication; the book, retitled *Northanger Abbey*, was published posthumously.

PERSUASION

Working Title: *The Elliots*
Written: 1816
Published: 1818

Jane Austen's final completed novel is a story of second chances. In the summer of 1806, Anne Elliot became engaged to Frederick Wentworth, a newly promoted naval officer waiting for a ship of his own. Under pressure from snobbish relatives who consider a half-pay officer not good enough for a baronet's daughter, and herself convinced that a wife will hold Wentworth back in his career, Anne reluctantly breaks off the engagement.

Eight years later, circumstances have changed: Anne's father, a "foolish, spendthrift baronet," is so much in debt that he must let the family estate and move to Bath. The house is leased by an admiral, coincidentally married to Captain Wentworth's sister, and Wentworth, who has made a fortune in the war and is still angry over the broken engagement, arrives for a visit. Anne, her own youthful bloom lost from eight years of unhappiness and regret, must watch while he flirts with two pretty young girls. A tragic event brings them together for a short time, but she leaves for Bath thinking he is lost to her forever, until circumstances change and love gets a second chance.

Jane Austen called this novel *The Elliots* and finished it less than a year before her death. In the first draft of the final chapters, Wentworth is jealous when the rumor mill has Anne engaged to her rich cousin; when Anne tells him that the gossip is untrue, they become engaged. Jane was dissatisfied with this ending and rewrote it, creating the classic scene in which Wentworth pours out his heart in a letter, apologizing and asking if it is not too late. The "cancelled chapters," as they are known, are now on display at the British Library, the only manuscript of the six major novels still extant. The novel, retitled *Persuasion*, was published posthumously in 1818 in a four-volume set with *Northanger Abbey*.

OTHER WORKS BY JANE AUSTEN

Many of these works were not published until the twentieth century, most as part of the Oxford Illustrated Editions edited by R. W. Chapman.

The "Juvenilia": Three notebooks into which Jane copied stories that she wrote when she was a young girl. The stories have a great deal of violence, death, and drunkenness but—or perhaps partly as a result—are extremely funny and show a precocious storytelling skill while parodying the conventions of contemporary fiction.

The History of England: "By a Partial, Prejudiced, and Ignorant Historian." A parody of serious histories, this short work gives brief, humorous overviews of the reign of each British monarch from Henry IV through Charles I. Cassandra Austen added illustrations of the various kings and queens. The manuscript is in the possession of the British Library and facsimile editions with the illustrations are widely available.

Lady Susan: A novella in letters; the title character is an amoral, manipulative sociopath who uses others indiscriminately, somewhat reminiscent of Madame de Merteuil of *Les Liaisons Dangereuses*. Jane Austen never attempted to publish it, perhaps because of the rather shocking subject matter, but technically it is brilliantly executed. It was first published in the second edition of J. E. Austen-Leigh's *Memoir*.

The Watsons: A rather darker version of *Pride and Prejudice*, this incomplete work sets up the story of the Watson sisters, three of whom are trying very hard to get married, as they have no mother and a sickly clergyman father who will leave them with nothing when he dies. Cassandra Austen later told family members that Jane's plan was that Mr. Watson would die in the course of the story and that the heroine, Emma Watson, would have to choose between marriage for money and position or for affection. Jane abandoned the story around the time of her father's death in 1805; perhaps the story of the orphaned daughters of a clergyman struck too close to home.

Sanditon: Jane Austen worked on this novel until a few months before her death, completing twelve chapters. The heroine, Charlotte Heywood, is invited to a small seaside town called Sanditon, which the inhabitants are trying to promote as a resort town. The characters gather, including the members of the Parker family: the eldest Mr. Parker, who is the main promoter of the town; his two sisters, Susan and Diana, and youngest brother, Arthur, all determined hypochondriacs; and his younger brother Sidney, of whom we have only a tantalizing glimpse, and who seems destined to be the hero of the piece. Brilliantly ironic and savagely funny, *Sanditon* might have been Jane Austen's finest novel had she lived to finish it.

CONTEMPORARY
JANE AUSTEN

Nearly two hundred years after her death, Jane Austen is more popular than ever. Film adaptations, biographies, sequels, retellings, an action figure—Janeites can't get enough of their favorite writer, and publishers and Hollywood are happy to oblige.

FILM ADAPTATIONS

While there were various television versions of Jane Austen's novels produced throughout the twentieth century, 1995 saw the "golden age" of Jane Austen adaptations, with an enormously popular BBC miniseries of *Pride and Prejudice*, starring Jennifer Ehle and Colin Firth in the lead roles, and a major motion picture of *Sense and Sensibility*, directed by Ang Lee and starring Emma Thompson (who won an Academy Award for writing the screenplay) and Kate Winslet. Other film and television adaptations of *Persuasion*, *Emma*, and *Mansfield Park* followed, the latter a controversial postmodern interpretation that brought filming of Austen novels to a screeching halt for several years. A second wave of Jane on film kicked off in 2005 with *Bride and Prejudice*, a contemporary Bollywood-style musical adaptation of *Pride and Prejudice*, and the first major motion picture adaptation of *Pride and Prejudice* since 1940, starring Keira Knightley and Matthew Macfadyen in the lead roles. The films listed are either available for purchase on DVD or in production at press time.

SENSE AND SENSIBILITY
1981: BBC television series, starring Irene Richard as Elinor and Tracey Childs as Marianne
1995: Columbia Pictures, starring Emma Thompson as Elinor and Kate Winslet as Marianne
2007: BBC television series, from a script by Andrew Davies

PRIDE AND PREJUDICE
1940: MGM, starring Greer Garson as Elizabeth and Laurence Olivier as Mr. Darcy
1980: BBC television series, starring Elizabeth Garvie as Elizabeth and David Rintoul as Mr. Darcy
1995: BBC/A&E television series, starring Jennifer Ehle as Elizabeth and Colin Firth as Mr. Darcy
2005: Working Title Films, starring Keira Knightley as Elizabeth and Matthew Macfadyen as Mr. Darcy

MANSFIELD PARK
1983: BBC television series, starring Sylvestra Le Touzel as Fanny and Nicholas Farrell as Edmund
1999: Miramax, starring Frances O'Connor as Fanny and Jonny Lee Miller as Edmund
2007: ITV television film, starring Billie Piper as Fanny and Blake Riston as Edmund

EMMA
1972: BBC television series, starring Doran Godwin as Emma and John Carson as Mr. Knightley
1996: Miramax, starring Gwyneth Paltrow as Emma and Jeremy Northam as Mr. Knightley
1996: ITV/A&E television film, starring Kate Beckinsale as Emma and Mark Strong as Mr. Knightley

Northanger Abbey

1986: BBC/A&E television film, starring Katharine Schlesinger as Catherine and Peter Firth as Henry
2007: ITV television film starring Felicity Jones as Catherine and JJ Feild as Henry

Persuasion

1971: BBC television version, starring Anne Firbank as Anne and Bryan Marshall as Captain Wentworth
1995: Sony Classics/Masterpiece Theatre, starring Amanda Root as Anne and Ciarán Hinds as Captain Wentworth
2007: ITV television film starring Sally Hawkins as Anne and Rupert Penry-Jones as Captain Wentworth

Biographical Films

2007: *Becoming Jane*, Ecosse Films, starring Anne Hathaway as Jane Austen and James McAvoy as Tom Lefroy
2007: *Miss Austen Regrets*, BBC television series

And Now for Something Completely Different . . .

Some filmmakers have recreated Jane Austen's stories in the present day, often in specific cultural settings that mimic the "three or four families in a country village" that was Jane Austen's preferred milieu.

Clueless, **Paramount Pictures, 1995:** A contemporary adaptation of *Emma*, written and directed by Amy Heckerling, starring Alicia Silverstone.

Kandukondain Kandukondain (**"I Have Found It"**), **Sri Surya Films, 2000:** Tamil-language Bollywood adaptation of *Sense and Sensibility*, starring Aishwarya Rai.

Pride and Prejudice: ***A Latter-Day Comedy***, **Excel Entertainment, 2003:** A contemporary "Mollywood" (set in the Mormon community) adaptation of *Pride and Prejudice*, starring Kam Heskin and Orlando Seale.

Bridget Jones's Diary, **Miramax, 2003**: Sometimes claimed as a modern adaptation of *Pride and Prejudice*, the film adaptation is so different from the original book by Helen Fielding that much of the P&P feeling is lost, despite Colin Firth's patented Darcy smolder.

Bride and Prejudice, **Miramax, 2005**: A contemporary Bollywood-style musical adaptation, directed by Gurinder Chadha, starring Aishwarya Rai and Martin Henderson.

Wishbone: **"Furst Impressions" and "Pup Fiction"**: Wishbone was a PBS television series for children in the 1990s, featuring a Jack Russell terrier called Wishbone, who would act out stories from classic literature alongside human costars to impart a life lesson to the young viewers. Two of Jane Austen's novels were adapted for the series: *Pride and Prejudice* became an episode called "Furst Impressions" and *Northanger Abbey* became an episode called "Pup Fiction." Wishbone is our favorite Henry Tilney on film.

SEQUELS, RETELLINGS, AND OTHER PARALITERATURE

Since Jane Austen first wrote her novels, readers have become so attached to the characters that they have wanted to know what happened to them after the action of the novels ended. In James Edward Austen-Leigh's memoir, he reveals that Jane told her nieces and nephews stories about their favorites to satisfy their curiosity; others have drawn their own conclusions and committed their stories to the page with varying degrees of success and popularity among Janeites.

Unsurprisingly, *Pride and Prejudice* has inspired most of these stories, including sequels, retellings of the original from another character's point of view (particularly Darcy's), retellings set in modern times, and even a series of mysteries featuring Mr. and Mrs. Darcy as sleuths. Jane herself is the detective in a series of mysteries by Stephanie Barron, and novelist Karen Joy Fowler's novel *The Jane Austen Book Club* is a contemporary comedy of manners about a book club that reads only Austen. There are several completions each of *The Watsons* and *Sanditon*, and the two Bridget Jones novels were inspired by Jane Austen novels (*Pride and Prejudice* and *Persuasion*). Jane Austen fan fiction communities flourish on the Internet, and some of the authors have published their work. Some sequels and fan fiction even follow the characters into previously uncharted Austen territory: the bedroom. There are so many Austen completions and continuations that a bibliography has been published: *After Jane* by Jennifer Scott.

RESOURCES

WEB SITES
AustenBlog (www.austenblog.com): News and commentary about Jane Austen in popular culture.

Molland's (www.mollands.net): An archival resource site for fans of Jane Austen, including searchable e-texts of the novels, an archive of illustrations and out-of-copyright e-texts about Jane and her work, a comprehensive links listing, and interactive areas.

The Republic of Pemberley (www.pemberley.com): The biggest and best-known Austen Web site, hosting busy and popular discussion forums as well as the Jane Austen Information Page.

Austen.com (www.austen.com): Hosts the Derbyshire Writers' Guild, a fan fiction archive and writers' community, as well as other e-texts and forums for writers of non-Austen fiction.

E-MAIL DISCUSSION LISTS
Austen-L (http://listserv.mcgill.ca/archives/austen-l.html): The original Jane Austen mailing list.

Janeites (http://groups.yahoo.com/group/janeites): A moderated e-mail discussion list.

JACastellano (http://espanol.groups.yahoo.com/group/jacastellano/): A Spanish-language Jane Austen discussion list.

JANE AUSTEN SOCIETIES

The Jane Austen Society of North America (www.jasna.org)

The Jane Austen Society (United Kingdom) (www.janeausten soci.freeuk.com)

The Jane Austen Society of Australia (www.jasa.net.au)

The Jane Austen Society of Melbourne (home.vicnet. net.au/~janeaust)

The Jane Austen Society of Buenos Aires, Argentina (www.janeaustenba.org)

There also are Austen societies in New Zealand and Japan.

PLACES TO VISIT

Jane Austen's House Museum, Chawton, Hampshire (www.janeaustenmuseum.org.uk): The display includes items owned, used, and made by Jane Austen and her family. The museum can be reached from London by public transportation and should not be missed by any Jane Austen fan. Take extra money for the gift shop! The parish church, where the Austen family members are buried, is a short walk down the road and welcomes visitors.

St. Nicholas's Church, Steventon, Hampshire: Jane Austen's church for the first twenty-five years of her life; her father, two of her brothers, and a nephew all took turns as rector. Other than the church, there are virtually no buildings in Steventon that Jane would have known, but it is a beautiful, peaceful place and positively hums with Austen vibes. It is not easy to get to, though Hidden Britain Tours (www.hiddenbritaintours.co.uk)

will drive visitors to Steventon and the sites that Jane would have known in the surrounding area.

The Jane Austen Centre, Bath (www.janeausten.co.uk): The center displays scenes of Bath when Jane Austen would have been living there (1801–1805) and has a tea room and well-stocked gift shop. The city of Bath is a wonderful place to visit for Janeites—you meet her characters around nearly every corner. The center also organizes a Jane Austen Festival each year in the autumn.

Winchester Cathedral, Winchester, Hampshire: Jane Austen's grave is located in the North Aisle of the cathedral. The stone makes no mention of her books, though Jane's nephew, James Edward Austen-Leigh, used the proceeds of his *Memoir of Jane Austen* to erect a memorial plaque. The house where she died is on College Street, a short walk away from the cathedral. It is marked with a blue plaque. It is not open to the public.

LIBRARIES AND ARCHIVES

The Jane Austen Collection at the Julia Rogers Library, Goucher College, Baltimore, Maryland (www.goucher. edu/x10707.xml): The best collection of Austeniana in existence, and much of it has been scanned and put online.

Chawton House Library, Chawton, Hampshire (www.chawton. org): Located in the former Great House of Edward Austen's estate at Chawton (just down the road from Jane Austen's House), this library and study centre preserves books written by British women between 1600 to 1830, a previously under-served literary niche. The library has very limited public hours.

SELECTED BIBLIOGRAPHY

BIOGRAPHIES

Jane Austen, by Elizabeth Jenkins (London: Victor Gollancz, 1938): Out of print, but worth seeking out in a used-book shop or on the Internet for the lovely, lyrical writing; an excellent first Austen biography.

*Jane Austen: A Family Record, by William Austen-Leigh, Richard Arthur Austen-Leigh, and Deirdre Le Faye (Boston: G. K. Hall, 1989): The single most useful book in the Jane Austen library.

Jane Austen: A Life, by Claire Tomalin (New York: Alfred A. Knopf, 1997): A well-written, readable biography.

Jane Austen: Her Life, by Park Honan (New York: St. Martin's Press, 1987): An insightful and informative work.

*Jane Austen, the Parson's Daughter, by Irene Collins (London: Hambledon Press, 1998): An examination of Jane Austen's life in Steventon and the effect it had on her growth as an author.

Jane Austen: The Woman, by George Holbert Tucker (New York: St. Martin's Press, 1994): A collection of essays about various aspects of Jane Austen's life.

---

*Works marked with an asterisk were consulted by the author in the writing of this book.

*_A History of Jane Austen's Family_, by George Holbert Tucker (Gloucestershire: Sutton Publishing, 1998): An excellent overview of Jane's parents, siblings, and ancestors that gives context to her life and work.

INFORMATION ABOUT JANE AUSTEN'S NOVELS AND WORLD

*_Jane Austen Fashion_, by Penelope Byrd (Ludlow, UK: Excellent Press, 1999).

*_Jane Austen and the Clergy_, by Irene Collins (London: Hambledon Press, 1994).

*_A Jane Austen Household Book_, by Peggy Hickman (North Pomfret, Vermont: David & Charles, 1977).

A Fine Brush on Ivory, by Richard Jenkyns (Oxford: Oxford University Press, 2004).

*_Jane Austen's World_, by Maggie Lane (London: Carlton Books, 1996).

*_Jane Austen: The World of Her Novels_, by Deirdre Le Faye (London: Frances Lincoln, 2002).

*_Jane Austen's Letters_, Third Edition, edited by Deirdre Le Faye (Oxford: Oxford University Press, 1995).

*Card Games, by John McLeod (www.pagat.com).

*David Parlett (Games Etc.), by David Parlett (www.david parlett.co.uk).

Jane Austen and the Navy, by Brian Southam (London: Hambledon and London, 2000).

Jane Austen In Style, by Susan Watkins (London and New York: Thames and Hudson, 1990).

GLOSSARY

Apothecary: Dispensed medication at the direction of a physician or surgeon. In remote country villages that did not have a physician, the apothecary was often the only source of medical advice. He would have been called "Mr. Perry" rather than "Doctor."

Banns: Public notice of intention to marry, read in the engaged couple's respective parish churches three times before their marriage.

Baronet: A commoner with a hereditary title; he would have been styled as "Sir Walter Elliot" and addressed as "Sir Walter"; a baronet's wife was styled as "Lady Elliot." Baronets were not peers and did not sit in the House of Lords.

Barouche: A carriage drawn by four to six horses, with room for six passengers (four on two seats facing one another, plus two more on the driver's box). The top folded back from the front like the top of a convertible automobile. The top of a **barouche-landau** folded back from the middle.

Barrister: An attorney who argued cases before a court of law. Barristers did not accept direct payment for their services, as they were gentlemen and did not engage in trade; **solicitors** contracted cases and acted as middlemen for payment.

Bluestocking: A woman who took a great interest in literary and intellectual pursuits. The name comes from the Bluestocking Society, a mid-eighteenth-century women's literary society.

Chaise: A closed carriage suitable for two to three passengers, without a driver's box, drawn by two to four horses that were directed by one or more postilions riding on the lead horses. A **post-chaise** was hired for long-distance travel and would collect fresh horses from posting inns as needed so the journey could continue uninterrupted.

Curricle: A fast, sporty two-wheeled open carriage drawn by two horses; it seated two and was driven by one of the riders.

Chemisette: A half-shirt, rather like a dickey, worn under a gown to cover the cleavage in daytime and give a gown a different look.

Cobb: A breakwater wall along the harbor's edge in the town of Lyme

Regis, located on the southern coast of England. Visitors often prome-naded along the Cobb to enjoy the sea air and views (and still do).

Curate: A priest hired to administer sacraments in a parish in the absence of the rector or vicar. He was paid only a salary, usually very small, and was not entitled to any of the parish tithes.

Direction: Refers to the address of the recipient on a letter.

Doctor: In Jane Austen's novels, a gentleman addressed as "Doctor" is usually a clergyman—a doctor of divinity—rather than a physician.

Doctor's Commons: A society of doctors of civil and canon law in London and the location of the ecclesiastical courts, which had jurisdic-tion over all legal matters to do with marriage. One procured a special license for marriage from Doctor's Commons.

Enlightenment: An eighteenth-century philosophical movement that espoused human reason as the proper basis for government and ethics.

Entailment: A legal contract dictating that an estate was to be inherited by the eldest male descendant in each generation. Such contracts kept estates from being broken up among several heirs.

Esquire: A style used to refer to a man from a family that had an official coat of arms (i.e., "Fitzwilliam Darcy, Esq."). The style generally indi-cated a man from an old and very good family.

Evangelicals: Members of a religious movement that emphasized Biblical infallibility and accepting Christ as one's personal savior.

Family living: See *living*; a family living was bestowed on a clergyman by his father or another relative.

Fichu: A triangular piece of netting or lace a woman tied around her shoulders or tucked into her bodice for modesty.

Fish: Betting chips shaped like fish used for card games.

Franking: Practice in which a member of Parliament signed, or "franked," a letter so its recipient did not have to pay for postage.

Funds, The: Investment by purchase of shares of a particular institution (for instance, the Royal Navy) that provided the investor with a regular income of about 3 to 5 percent on the capital each year.

Gambling hell: A private gaming establishment for gentlemen only, where many a fine fortune was lost.

Gentleman: A generic term for a man of good family. The more fastidi-ous used the term only to refer to those who owned property.

Gentry: Members of nonaristocratic, landowning families, including those who did not own property themselves (i.e., younger sons). Members of the gentry generally did not work for a living, except in a few acceptable professions.

Georgian: The era encapsulating the reigns of George I through George IV, 1714–1830. The **Regency** is a separate era within the Georgian era.

Gig: A fast, sporty, two-wheeled open carriage drawn by one horse that could accommodate two passengers and was driven by one of its riders.

Glebe: Farmland that formed part of the compensation of a clergyman, which he could farm himself or rent out and keep the profits.

Grand tour: After completing his formal education, a young gentleman would spend from six months to several years traveling the European continent to acquire polished manners and further his cultural education.

Hack carriage: A carriage hired from a livery stable for a short time; for instance, to take one back and forth to a ball.

Ha-ha: A sunken ditch used to keep livestock confined to a particular area without putting up fences that would spoil a view.

Interest: When used in relation to naval officers, referred to the patronage of senior officers or other powerful or influential individuals that an officer employed to advance in his career.

Knight: A man who had received a title from the monarch, usually for some special service rendered. The title was not hereditary. He was styled as "Sir William Lucas" and addressed as "Sir William." His wife was styled "Lady Lucas."

Knotting: A handicraft in which silk or cotton was tied in knots about a quarter of an inch apart to form a trim that resembled a string of beads or French knots. These were later fashioned into fringe to edge curtains or sewn onto fabric that was used to upholster furniture.

Lady: A generic term used to indicate a woman of a good family. Used as a title, it indicated the wife of a peer, baronet, or knight (properly addressed as "Lady Russell") or the daughter of a peer (addressed as "Lady Catherine").

Landaulet: A four-wheeled open carriage similar to a phaeton but with a box for a driver up front.

Linen-draper: A store that sold fabric and trimming for making clothing; sometimes also sold accessories such as gloves.

Living: A clerical appointment to a parish church in which a clergyman collected tithes or was paid a salary. The power to bestow the living of a particular parish was a possession that could be inherited, purchased, and sold. Clergymen networked with wealthy landowners who sometimes had several livings in their gift.

Mantua-maker: A dressmaker. A mantua was a type of gown popular in the late seventeenth and early eighteenth century, and while the style went out of fashion, the name for their creators stuck.

Marine Parade: A pavement walk in a seaside resort, usually with a view of the sea, where fashionable residents and visitors promenaded.

Marriage agreement: A prenuptial agreement detailing the disposition of any fortune that a woman brought into a marriage and the financial arrangements for her and her children.

Mending a pen: Pens were made of quill feathers needed to be sharpened or "mended" regularly with a penknife.

Methodists: Members of a religious movement that grew in reaction to the Enlightenment principles of natural religion and deism. The Methodists espoused Biblical infallibility and a more orthodox approach to Christianity.

Miser's purse: A small purse for holding banknotes and coins. It was made as a long tube with an opening in the middle part and two rings that slid along the tube. One moved the rings to either side of the opening to insert money and then slid the rings back to keep the money inside at either end. Such purses were used by both men and women. When Mr. Bingley refers to ladies "netting a purse" in *Pride and Prejudice*, this is the sort of purse he means, not a reticule.

Napoleonic Wars: Officially, the campaigns fought by the French army from the time Napoleon Bonaparte became Emperor of France in 1799 through the Battle of Waterloo in 1815, with a brief break in 1814 while Napoleon was confined on the island of Elba. The term also sometimes is used to include the war between France and England and their various allies that occurred between the time of the beheading of Louis XVI of France in 1793 and the Peace of Amiens from 1802 to 1803.

Negus: Hot mulled (spiced) wine that was often served in the evening and during supper at balls.

Netting: A handicraft in which thread is wound onto a netting needle, wrapped around a gauge, and tied in knots at regular intervals to form a mesh fabric. Very fine mesh was used to make misers' purses.

Pattern gown: A gown that could easily be taken apart and copied onto another piece of fabric as the guide for another gown.

Peer: A member of the House of Lords, including (in ascending order of rank) barons, viscounts, earls, marquises, and dukes. All but dukes were addressed as "Lord Dalrymple" and their wives as "Lady Dalrymple." In a few very rare cases, a peerage could be inherited by a woman, but they almost always fell along the male line.

Pelisse: A woman's overcoat.

Petticoat: A gown worn under a lighter or open gown. A **waist petticoat** was like a long half-slip and was worn for warmth or modesty.

Phaeton: A four-wheeled open carriage with seating for two to four people that was driven by a passenger and drawn by one to four horses or ponies. The body of a **high-perch phaeton** was suspended above the undercarriage, making it less stable, but faster and more maneuverable for experienced drivers.

Physician: A formally educated medical man who interpreted symptoms and prescribed treatment. Physicians were gentlemen and therefore did not perform surgery or any tasks classified as "work" in the standards of the day.

Pianoforte: A piano.

Picturesque, The: Introduced by clergyman William Gilpin's series of travel journals, a new idea of aesthetics in which the beauties of nature became more desirable than regulation forced upon nature by man.

Pin money: The money allotted to a woman in her marriage agreement for her personal expenses.

Professions: Referred to the few vocations open to gentlemen: the army, the navy, the church, the law, and medicine.

Public assembly: A ball open to the public to attend, as long as they had paid the subscription fee. Many towns had special assembly rooms set aside for this purpose.

Public school: A boarding school that any boy of good family could attend—for a fee. They were not supported by taxes but were "public" in the sense that the boys were taught in classes rather than receiving private one-on-one tutoring.

Pump room: As a generic term, an establishment in a spa town where one went to drink spring water. In Bath, *the* Pump Room was located near the Abbey and was one of the most popular locations in the town for socializing. Other pump rooms in Bath included the Hetling Pump Room, where members of the Austen family drank the water.

Ragout: A stewed or baked dish.

Rector: A clergyman or layman who collected the great tithes, or 10 percent of the profits from cereal crops in a parish. Lay rectors hired a vicar or curate to administer sacraments in the parish.

Regency: From 1810 through 1820, the Prince of Wales ruled England as Prince Regent in the stead of his father, George III, who suffered from dementia. The term often is used generically to refer to the early nineteenth century.

Reticule: A small handbag.

Royal Crescent: A semicircular terrace of homes in Bath, designed by John Wood the Younger, completed in 1774. It was the showplace of Georgian Bath and an exclusive address. Many of the residents of Bath liked to promenade along the pavement of the Crescent on Sunday after church.

Set: A group of dancers in a country dance, as well as the dances that they perform together.

Shift: A woman's undergarment, constructed like a sack dress, intended to keep clothing cleaner by keeping them from direct contact with the skin.

Squire: The principal landowner in a village; Mr. Bennet, Mr. Darcy, and Mr. Knightley all were the squires of their respective villages.

Special license: A license that granted a couple dispensation from marrying before noon, in their parish church, and eliminating the need to publish the banns.

Spencer: A short overcoat made like the bodice and sleeves of a gown.

Spinster: A legal term for an unmarried woman; a trifle uncomplimentary when used in everyday speech.

Stagecoach: A public conveyance in which one traveled in a large group, stopping at predetermined locations.

Stays: A corset.

Surgeon: A medical practitioner who could set bones and perform operations. Surgeons were not considered gentlemen and were not addressed as Doctor, but as Mister.

Syllabub: Cream whipped with fruit juice; it could be drunk or eaten with a spoon.

Tambour: A style of embroidery in which a fine hook was used to draw thread through fabric that was stretched over an embroidery hoop, resulting in what looked like a chain stitch. An ancestor of crocheting.

Ton, The: Fashionable society. *Ton* without the article referred to polished manners; one was spoken of as having "good *ton*."

Tithes: A set percentage of income required to be paid to a parish clergyman or lay rector. This payment constituted a clergyman's income along with profits from glebe land.

Vicar: A clergyman entitled to collect a parish's small tithes (10 percent of the profits from livestock and produce) or paid a salary by the rector.

Wafer: A gummed label that became sticky when moistened on one side; used to seal letters.

INDEX

ACKNOWLEDGMENTS

I'm tremendously grateful for all the help and support I had while writing this book. First I must express my groveling Mr. Collins-like gratitude to Melissa Wagner for wrangling my rampant Janeite geekiness into useful and readable form. Thanks to my Janeite Posse for their information, input, assistance, and support: Laura Boyle, Lorna Carton, Teresa Fields, Cinthia García Soria, Lorraine Hanaway, Robin Hutchinson, Karen Lee, Elizabeth Steele, Allison Thompson, Kathleen Walker-Meikle, Diane Wilkes, and Jennifer Winski. Thanks to Jim McCarthy for taking care of business so I could just write. Thanks to the readers of AustenBlog for keeping me on my toes, and to all those who have read and commented on my Austen stories and essays over the years. Thanks to my family for the warm encouragement: Bill and Betty Sullivan, Rita and Dennis Kirkwood, Jerry Sullivan, and Megan and Billy Horan. Thanks to my coworkers for putting up with my sleep-deprived crankiness while writing this book and for not telling me to shut UP already about Jane Austen, or at least not as often as they should. Thanks to my Horatian friends, who always have my back, even though I've neglected them shamefully while working on this book. Thanks to Kevin Kosbab and everyone at Quirk for making the book, like Henry Tilney, perfect, or very near it. Thanks to Kathryn Rathke for the gorgeous illustrations and to Bryn Ashburn for making the book beautiful. And most importantly, thanks to Jane Austen, for writing the books that have brought me so much pleasure and inspiration and for reminding me that "an artist cannot do anything slovenly."

ABOUT THE AUTHOR

Margaret C. Sullivan is the editrix of AustenBlog.com, which catalogs and comments upon the collision of Jane Austen with popular culture, and one of the creators of Molland's (www.mollands.net), an archive and community Web site for Jane Austen readers. She is a life member of the Jane Austen Society of North America and is a member of the board of JASNA's Eastern Pennsylvania/Delaware Valley Region as well as the region's webmaster. She works for an international law firm as their Web content coordinator and spends her nearly nonexistent free time attempting to convince the world that Henry Tilney is way cooler than that Darcy fellow. She lives in the suburbs of Philadelphia, which she wishes were much closer to Bath, and is a graduate of Penn State University. Her personal Web site can be found at www.tilneysandtrapdoors.com.

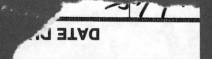